MAKE IT YOUR OWN

MAKE IT YOUR OWN

Recipes & Inspiration for the Creative Cook

Jamie Miller

CUMBERLAND HOUSE
NASHVILLE, TENNESSEE

MAKE IT YOUR OWN
PUBLISHED BY CUMBERLAND HOUSE PUBLISHING
431 Harding Industrial Drive
Nashville, Tennessee 37211

Cover design: JulesRules Design
Book design: Mary Sanford

Library of Congress Cataloging-in-Publication Data
Miller, Jamie, 1963–
  Make it your own : recipes & inspiration for the creative cook / Jamie Miller.
      p. cm.
  Includes index.
  ISBN-13: 978-1-58182-593-0 (pbk. : alk. paper)
  ISBN-10: 1-58182-593-5 (pbk. : alk. paper)
  ISBN-13: 978-1-68336-801-4 (hc)
  1. Cookery. I. Title.
  TX652.M557 2007
  641.5—dc22

                                                          2007015335

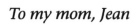

To my mom, Jean

CONTENTS

CONTENTS

MAKE IT YOUR OWN

HOW TO USE THIS BOOK

Make It Your Own: Recipes and Inspiration for the Creative Cook is a cookbook for people who love to spend time in the kitchen, creating unique and memorable meals to share with family and friends.

The book is brimming with interesting and delicious recipes that are sure to impress your dinner guests; but more importantly, it is designed to instill in you the ideas, inspiration and sense of adventure needed to take what's here and make it your own.

Part One of the book is comprised of recipes for the marinades, spice rubs, salsas, sauces, and more that are the building blocks for the hors d'oeuvre, entrée and side dish recipes that make up Part Two. Each of the recipes in Part One is followed by a section entitled *Tried & True* and another entitled *Something New.*

Tried & True is simply a listing of each recipe within the book that utilizes that particular sauce or marinade along with the page number on which it is located. For example, if you find yourself dying to try the Pancetta-Corn Salsa on page 60, you can quickly find all of the recipes within the book that make use of that salsa by looking under *Tried & True.*

Something New includes a few ideas for other ways in which you might use that marinade or salsa. These are not actual recipes, but rather simple ideas to help get your own creative juices flowing. It is my hope that you will find recipes in Part One that you absolutely love and will come up with all sorts of your own additional uses for them!

Part Two of the book contains dozens of recipes for hors d'oeuvres, entrées, and side dishes. While all of the recipes here are delicious and impressive enough for entertaining, none are difficult, and most can be completed in an hour or two. With a little advance planning, many of the entrée recipes can even be whipped up on a hectic weeknight.

All of the recipes in Part Two are followed by two sections: *Classic Combos* and *Daring Pairings*. In these sections, I give you complete directions for altering the original recipe to come up with a completely new dish.

Classic Combos, as you might expect, are recipes with more traditional flavor combinations. An example of a *Classic Combo* is the Mustard Seed Salmon with Lemon-Dill Aioli on page 46. While the seed crust and the aioli might be new to you, the flavors of mustard, dill, and lemon are often paired with salmon. These are the "safe" recipes . . . the ones you serve your mother-in-law!

The *Daring Pairing* recipes are where we really start to have some fun. These recipe variations might include unusual flavor combinations, exotic or ethnic spices and ingredients, or maybe just interesting ways of combining recipe elements. An example of a *Daring Pairing* is the Jamaican Jerk Lettuce Wraps with Savory Mango-Papaya Salsa on page 70. I've taken what is traditionally an Asian dish, lettuce wraps, and filled them with Jamaican spiced meat and a Caribbean-style fruit salsa.

Following are a few tips for successfully making the *Classic Combo* and *Daring Pairing* variations:

- You may want to consider making the original recipe before making the variations, particularly for the more involved recipes, to ensure that you are comfortable with the preparation and cooking techniques.

- Read the entire original recipe before beginning, to make sure you are familiar with the cooking procedure and have all of the necessary ingredients.

- Read any supplemental recipes that you'll be using (e.g. a salsa or sauce) to make sure you know how long it will take to prepare and that you have all of the ingredients.

- Take marinating time into account if needed.

- Have your ingredients prepped and accessible.

- Changes to the original recipe are listed in the order in which they occur. Make sure you don't skip any steps.

- If the instructions say to replace one ingredient with another, the new ingredient should be in the same quantity, unless otherwise specified. The new ingredient should also be added to the recipe at the same time and cooked and handled in the same manner.

- Don't omit anything from the original recipe unless the variation specifically says to "omit" or "replace" the ingredient.

- Don't forget to season with salt and pepper at the appropriate times throughout recipe preparation.

- Most of the recipes contain some type of fresh herb. Use extra sprigs for garnishing dinner plates and serving platters.

- While I hope you will enjoy all of the recipes in this book, my true desire is that you will be inspired to mix and match the recipes here to come up with delicious dishes and menus that are all your own. I have even included a few pages at the back of the book for you to record these *Creative Couplings,* so get in the kitchen and have some fun!

A FEW FAVORITE INGREDIENTS & TECHNIQUES

Aleppo Pepper

The Aleppo pepper is a small, reddish-brown chile from Turkey and the Middle East. It has a deliciously deep, smoky and somewhat tart flavor with moderate heat. Find Aleppo pepper at Middle Eastern markets or at www.penzeys.com or www.deananddeluca.com.

ASIAN INGREDIENTS

All of the Asian ingredients used here can be found at well-stocked supermarkets, Asian markets, and online at www.ethnicgrocer.com.

Asian Chile Sauce comes in many varieties. All contain chiles, salt and oil. Some varieties also add garlic and other flavorings. With the exception of sweet chile sauce, which is a condiment used as a dipping sauce for eggrolls and spring rolls, all of the chile sauces and pastes can be used interchangeably in the recipes here. My favorite chile sauce is Sriracha, a lightly sweetened version that is less hot than the others. It is bright orange, comes in squeeze bottles, and is very inexpensive. Have fun with Sriracha by squirting decorative designs on dinner plates and platters.

Asian Sesame Oil, also called toasted sesame oil, is a dark, richly flavored oil used for flavoring rather than for cooking. I like to keep it in the refrigerator to ensure freshness.

Chinese Five-Spice Powder is a wonderfully fragrant spice mix used frequently in Chinese stir-fries. While the five spices used vary from brand to brand, it typically contains cinnamon, star anise, ginger, cloves and fennel. Find it in the spice section of supermarkets, at Asian markets, or online at www.penzeys.com or www.deananddeluca.com.

Fish Sauce is a condiment/ingredient made from salted and fermented anchovies that adds an unmistakable South Asian flavor to foods. Both the Thai and Vietnamese versions are good.

Hoisin Sauce is a flavorful Chinese condiment/ingredient made from soybean paste, sugar, garlic, peppers, vinegar, and spices.

Lemongrass is a fragrant, citrusy stalk used in Thai cooking. Use just the tender inner bulb and chop finely. Grated lemon zest can be substituted in a pinch, but the flavor will not be the same.

Mirin is a sweetened rice wine used frequently in Japanese cooking. If unavailable, substitute 1 tablespoon sake or dry sherry plus 1 teaspoon sugar for each tablespoon mirin.

Miso is a fermented soybean paste used in Japanese cooking. The different types vary in color, saltiness, and depth of flavor. Recipes in the book call for both white (shiro miso), which is lighter in flavor, and dark (aka miso), which is saltier and more intense.

Panko is a dry Japanese breadcrumb that is lighter and flakier than typical dried breadcrumbs. It makes a terrific crunchy coating for fried foods and lightens burgers, such as the salmon and tuna burgers here. If unavailable, substitute lightly toasted fresh breadcrumbs.

Pickled Ginger, also called sushi ginger, is a sweet, salty, and crunchy condiment usually served with sushi. Find it in the Asian section or the refrigerated section of your supermarket.

Sake, also known as Japanese rice wine, is used in marinades and dipping sauces and for cooking. It can be found in most liquor stores and wine shops. If unavailable, substitute dry sherry.

Toasted Sesame Seeds—While you can certainly toast your own sesame seeds on an as-needed basis, I cheat a little and buy big jars of toasted sesame seeds at the Asian market. They are relatively inexpensive and will stay fresh for many months if kept in the fridge.

Wasabi, also called Japanese horseradish, can be found as a paste in small tubes, or as a powder. I prefer the paste for the recipes in this book, as it is more flavorful and lends its pretty green color to condiments such as the Wasabi Mayo.

Double-Strength Tomato Paste

This is great when you want to add intensity to a dish without too much tomato flavor. It is imported from Italy and comes in airtight tubes that can be stored in the refrigerator for months without spoiling. It is available at most supermarkets with the regular canned tomato paste. If unavailable, substitute twice as much regular tomato paste in the recipes here

HERBS & SPICES

Fresh herbs are used extensively in recipes throughout the book, with dried herbs being used to a lesser extent. While I don't recommend substituting dried herbs in recipes that call for fresh, you can do so in a pinch, by using one-third as much of the dried herb. When the recipe is uncooked, such as a salad, salsa, or mayo, dried herbs generally do not make an acceptable substitute for fresh. A wide array of spices are also used throughout the book. While all of them should be available at well-stocked supermarkets, I also recommend trying the high-quality dried herbs and spices available from www.penzeys.com and www.deananddeluca.com.

Garam Masala   This is an incredibly aromatic and delicious Indian spice blend that usually contains coriander, pepper, cardamom, cinnamon, ginger, cloves, and more. Brands such as McCormick are widely available in supermarkets, but since ingredients can vary widely from brand to brand, you may want to try more than one to find your favorite. Find it at Indian markets or online at www.penzeys.com and www.deananddeluca.com.

Pancetta & Prosciutto   Pancetta is an unsmoked Italian bacon that is cured with salt, pepper, and other spices. It adds incredible flavor and depth to many of the recipes in the book. Thick-cut bacon can be substituted, but it has a higher proportion of fat, which should be drained off before proceeding with the recipe. Prosciutto is an unsmoked, salted, and air-cured Italian ham that is typically sold in paper thin slices. It can be eaten as is, sautéed in olive oil for a crispy topping, or used in countless ways in recipes. American made versions of both pancetta and prosciutto are widely available and can be used in all of the recipes in the book.

Roasted Garlic   You will see that many of the recipes in this book utilize roasted garlic. I just love its rich, mellow flavor! While it is available in jars at the grocery store; making your own is simple and much less expensive. Roast one head at a time, or do as I do and roast entire bagfuls at once. Preheat the oven to 375°. Peel the outermost papery skin from the garlic head. Slice off the top $1/4$-inch or so to expose the cloves. Place the garlic head on a sheet of heavy-duty foil, drizzle with a little extra virgin olive oil, wrap tightly, and roast for 45 minutes. Remove from the oven and allow to cool partially before unwrapping. Remove from the foil; squeeze the garlic flesh into a small bowl and mash with a fork.

To roast many heads at once, trim as above then place them all on a large baking sheet or pan. Drizzle with oil, cover tightly with foil, and roast at 375° for 1 hour. Allow to cool partially before removing foil, then squeeze garlic flesh into a food processor or mini-processor and purée. Divide the purée between small freezer bags or, better yet, small plastic containers that can be pulled directly from the freezer to the refrigerator every time you're running low. Store, airtight, in the refrigerator for up to 3 weeks or freeze for up to 6 months.

Roasted Red Peppers   Here is another ingredient you'll find used throughout the book. Its delicious, slightly smoky flavor enhances many recipes. While many bottled brands are available at the grocery store, it's easy to roast them yourself. Buy a bagful when you spot them at a good price or when the farmer's market offers them by the bushel! Roast them all at once and freeze in single-pepper portions. Here's how: Preheat the broiler. Hold the pepper up by the stem and cut off the four sides. Discard the core and trim any membranes from the pepper slices. Place the pepper slices, flesh side down, on a large baking sheet covered with foil. Flatten any rounded pieces with the palm of your hand. You can squeeze as many as will fit onto your baking sheet, as long as they don't overlap. Broil, about 5 or 6 inches from the flame, until they are almost completely blackened. You will want to check them every minute or so and remove them, one at a time, as they are blackened. Transfer the peppers to a ziplock bag or paper bag. Close the bag tightly and allow it to sit for 15 minutes. Remove the peppers from the bag and peel off the skins. They should slip right off; but it's fine if there are some small charred pieces of skin remaining. Lay 4 sections (1 pepper) atop each other on a sheet of plastic wrap and wrap tightly. Repeat with the remaining pepper sections and toss the whole batch in a big freezer bag, to pull out as needed. Store, airtight, in the refrigerator for up to 4 days or freeze for up to 6 months.

Sweet Smoked Paprika   Pimentón de la Vera is a sweet, smoked paprika from Spain that adds an undeniably Spanish flavor to a number of recipes in the book. La Chinata brand is available at gourmet grocers or online at www.tienda.com. Piment d'Esplet is a similar smoked paprika from the Basque region of France that is also delicious and can be used as a substitute for pimenton. Igo brand is available at gourmet grocers and some supermarkets.

Wine & Fortified Wine   I am a firm believer in the old adage, "If you wouldn't drink it, don't cook with it." When a recipe calls for dry red wine, you don't need to pull out your best Napa Valley Cabernet, but you should certainly use a tasty, fruity red that you would enjoy sipping. When recipes call for dry white wine, it is best to stay away from oak-aged wines, such as Chardonnay, and stick to light, crisp whites like Sauvignon Blanc and Pinot Grigio. Many of the recipes in the book also call for fortified wines such as port, sherry, Marsala, and Madeira. These wines add tremendous flavor to a wide variety of sauces and dishes, so once again, don't be tempted to buy the cheap stuff. Due to their higher alcohol content, open bottles can be kept, airtight, for quite some time. For maximum freshness, keep them in the refrigerator. Feel free to substitute similarly flavored wines (e.g. Marsala and Madeira) if you don't want to keep all of the varieties on hand. Just be sure that they also have a similar level of sweetness.

PART ONE

Marinades, Pastes, and Rubs

The marinades, pastes, and rubs in this section have flavors that span the globe. They provide a flavor base upon which many of the recipes in the book are built. While they pair beautifully with the salsas, sauces and other add-ons in the upcoming sections, they can also be used alone to add delicious and exotic flavors to easy weeknight meals.

Feel free to experiment with the recipes in this section; substituting different herbs, spices and aromatics based on your personal preferences and what ingredients you have on hand. Use the following guidelines for marinating, unless otherwise specified in a recipe:

- Marinate seafood and delicate fish for 30 to 60 minutes.
- Marinate firm-fleshed fish for 1 to 2 hours.
- Marinate poultry, pork chops, and pork tenderloin for 1 to 3 hours.
- Marinate steaks, lamb chops, and kabob meat for 2 to 4 hours.
- Marinate larger cuts of beef, pork, and lamb for 4 to 8 hours.

Thai Lemongrass Marinade

3   TABLESPOONS CHOPPED SCALLIONS

2   TABLESPOONS CHOPPED LEMONGRASS, INNER BULB ONLY

1^1/$_2$ TABLESPOONS CHOPPED FRESH GINGER

1^1/$_2$ TABLESPOONS CHOPPED FRESH GARLIC

2   TABLESPOONS SOY SAUCE

2   TABLESPOONS THAI OR VIETNAMESE FISH SAUCE

2   TABLESPOONS FRESH LIME JUICE

1^1/$_2$ TABLESPOONS LIGHT BROWN SUGAR

1   TABLESPOON ASIAN SESAME OIL

^{1}/$_2$ TABLESPOON ASIAN CHILE SAUCE

^{1}/$_4$ CUP CHOPPED FRESH CILANTRO

Combine all ingredients in a blender or mini-processor and purée. Makes about 1 cup.

Thai Coconut Marinade

1   RECIPE THAI LEMONGRASS MARINADE

^{1}/$_2$ CUP SWEETENED, SHREDDED COCONUT

Combine all ingredients in a blender or mini-processor and purée. Makes about 1^1/$_2$ cups.

Thai Orange-Coconut Marinade

1   RECIPE THAI COCONUT MARINADE
    JUICE AND GRATED ZEST FROM 1 MEDIUM
    ORANGE

Combine all ingredients in a blender or mini-processor and purée. Makes about 1^3/$_4$ cups.

Thai Basil Marinade

Replace the lemongrass in Thai Lemongrass Marinade with $1/4$ cup chopped fresh Thai basil or regular sweet basil. Reduce the amount of cilantro to 2 tablespoons. Purée as above. Makes about $1^1/4$ cups.

Notes

These marinades are great on all types of fish and seafood, as well as chicken, pork, and beef. Recipes make enough for 2 pounds of meat.

Tried & True

- Thai Coconut Chicken Sate with Peanut Sauce (page 137)
- Thai Lemongrass Beer Can Chicken (page 177)
- Thai Lemongrass Grilled Pork Tenderloin with Cucumber-Pineapple Salsa (page 186)
- Thai Lemongrass Lettuce Wraps with Spicy Peanut Dipping Sauce (page 207)
- Thai Coconut Lettuce Wraps with Cucumber-Pineapple Salsa (page 207)

Something New

- Marinate shrimp and scallops in Thai Orange-Coconut Marinade, skewer, and grill or broil.
- Marinate flank steak in Thai Lemongrass Marinade and grill or broil. Thinly slice and serve with lettuce leaves for wrapping. Boil reserved marinade for 3 minutes and use as a dipping sauce.
- Marinate salmon fillets in Thai Coconut Marinade and grill or broil. Top with grilled pineapple rings.

Teriyaki Marinade

1/4 CUP SOY SAUCE
1/4 CUP MIRIN
3 TABLESPOONS MINCED SCALLIONS
2 TABLESPOONS SAKE OR DRY SHERRY
2 TABLESPOONS LIGHT BROWN SUGAR

2 TEASPOONS MINCED FRESH GINGER
2 TEASPOONS MINCED FRESH GARLIC
1 TEASPOON ASIAN CHILE SAUCE OR RED PEPPER FLAKES

In a small bowl whisk together all ingredients. Makes about 1 cup.

Island Teriyaki Marinade

1/2 CUP PINEAPPLE JUICE
1/2 CUP MINCED SCALLIONS
6 TABLESPOONS SOY SAUCE
1/4 CUP MIRIN
1/4 CUP MINCED FRESH CILANTRO

3 TABLESPOONS LIGHT BROWN SUGAR
2 TABLESPOONS SAKE OR DRY SHERRY
4 TEASPOONS MINCED FRESH GINGER
2 TEASPOONS MINCED FRESH GARLIC
1 TEASPOON ASIAN CHILE SAUCE

In a small bowl whisk together all ingredients. Makes about 2 cups.

Orange-Sesame Teriyaki Marinade

1 RECIPE TERIYAKI MARINADE
1/2 CUP FRESH ORANGE JUICE
2 TABLESPOONS ASIAN SESAME OIL

2 TABLESPOONS SOY SAUCE
2 TABLESPOONS LIGHT BROWN SUGAR
1 TEASPOON GRATED ORANGE ZEST

In a small bowl whisk together all ingredients. Makes about 1 3/4 cups.

Notes

These marinades work well on seafood, fish, poultry, pork, beef, and even tofu. Recipes make enough for 2 to 3 pounds meat. To use these marinades for basting or glazing, remove meat and boil the marinade in a small saucepan for 2 to 3 minutes until slightly syrupy.

Tried & True

- Coconut-Corn Salsa (page 64)
- Island Teriyaki Shrimp Skewers (page 131)
- Orange-Sesame Grilled Salmon (page 155)
- Teriyaki Tuna Burgers with Cucumber-Pineapple Salsa (page 161)
- Teriyaki Grilled Sea Bass with Coconut-Corn Salsa (page 163)
- Teriyaki Sirloin with Coconut-Corn Salsa (page 203)
- Teriyaki Lettuce Wraps with Wasabi Ponzu (page 207)

Something New

- Marinate beef tenderloin cubes in any of the above marinades. Skewer, along with green pepper and red onion chunks and grill. Serve with Ponzu Dipping Sauce or Wasabi Ponzu (page 112).
- Baste grilled or oven-roasted asparagus with Orange-Sesame Teriyaki Marinade.
- Use any of the marinades as a sauce for stir-fried meats and vegetables or fried rice.

Korean-Style BBQ Marinade

$1/3$ CUP SOY SAUCE

2 TABLESPOONS MIRIN

2 TABLESPOONS DARK BROWN SUGAR

2 TABLESPOONS MINCED FRESH GARLIC

$1^1/2$ TABLESPOONS ASIAN SESAME OIL

$1^1/2$ TABLESPOONS ASIAN CHILE SAUCE

1 TABLESPOON MINCED FRESH GINGER

In a small bowl combine all ingredients. Whisk thoroughly until sugar is dissolved. Makes about 1 cup, or enough for $1^1/2$ pounds poultry, pork, or beef.

Miso-Mustard Marinade

$1/2$ CUP LIGHT (SHIRO) MISO

$1/2$ CUP MIRIN

2 TABLESPOONS SAKE OR DRY SHERRY

2 TABLESPOONS BROWN SUGAR

1 TABLESPOON CHINESE HOT MUSTARD

In a small bowl combine all ingredients. Whisk. Makes about $1^1/4$ cups, or enough for 2 pounds fish or seafood.

Tried & True

- Miso Grilled Salmon with Sesame-Scallion Gremolata (page 154)
- Miso Grilled Sea Bass with Edamame Salsa (page 163)
- Korean Beef & Pork Lettuce Wraps with Sesame-Soy Dipping Sauce (page 206)
- Korean BBQ Steak Roll (page 209)

Something New

- Mix Korean-Style BBQ Marinade into browned ground beef for Asian-flavored Sloppy Joes.
- Marinate meats and poultry in Korean-Style BBQ Marinade for stir-fries.
- Marinate bacon-wrapped scallops in Miso-Mustard Marinade for 1 hour; skewer and grill or broil for a tasty appetizer.
- Brush asparagus with Miso-Mustard Marinade during grilling or oven-roasting.

Mojo Marinade

3/4 CUP FRESH ORANGE JUICE

1/2 CUP CHOPPED SWEET ONION

1/4 CUP FRESH LIME JUICE

1/4 CUP GRAND MARNIER OR OTHER ORANGE LIQUEUR

1/4 CUP EXTRA VIRGIN OLIVE OIL

1/4 CUP SOY SAUCE

2 TABLESPOONS CHOPPED FRESH GARLIC

2 TABLESPOONS CHOPPED FRESH OREGANO OR 2 TEASPOONS DRIED

1 1/2 TEASPOONS GROUND CUMIN

1 1/2 TEASPOONS FRESHLY GROUND PEPPER

1 TEASPOON LIME ZEST

In a blender combine all ingredients and purée. Makes 2 cups.

Margarita Marinade

1/2 CUP MINCED SWEET ONION

1/2 CUP FRESH LIME JUICE

6 TABLESPOONS TEQUILA

1/4 CUP FROZEN ORANGE JUICE CONCENTRATE, THAWED

2 TABLESPOONS MINCED FRESH GARLIC

2 TABLESPOONS OLIVE OIL

2 TEASPOONS DRIED OREGANO (MEXICAN PREFERRED)

2 TEASPOONS CHIPOTLE CHILE POWDER

2 TEASPOONS GROUND CUMIN

1 1/2 TEASPOONS COARSE SEA SALT OR KOSHER SALT

1 TEASPOON FRESHLY GROUND PEPPER

In a blender combine all ingredients and purée. Makes 1 3/4 cups.

Notes

Both marinades are particularly delicious with fish and seafood but would make for tasty grilled chicken and pork as well. Due to the large amount of lime juice in both marinades, be sure not to let foods marinate for more than 1 to 2 hours unless otherwise stated in the recipes.

Tried & True

- Mojo Grilled Sea Bass with Floribbean Salsa (page 162)
- Margarita Swordfish with Tomato-Mango Salsa (page 164)
- Mojo Swordfish with Savory Caribbean Salsa (page 165)
- Citrus Swordfish Skewers with Chimichurri (page 167)

Something New

- Marinate shrimp in either marinade for 30 minutes, skewer, and grill or broil for an easy appetizer.
- Marinate chicken chunks in Mojo Marinade then grill, broil, or sauté and serve with cocktail picks and a bowl of Mojo Mayo (page 44) for dipping.

Rosemary-Lemon Marinade

$1/2$ CUP CHOPPED ONION

$1/2$ CUP EXTRA VIRGIN OLIVE OIL

$1/4$ CUP DRY WHITE WINE

JUICE AND GRATED ZEST OF 1 LEMON

3 TABLESPOONS CHOPPED FRESH ROSEMARY

$1^1/_2$ TABLESPOONS CHOPPED FRESH GARLIC

$1/2$ TEASPOON COARSE SEA SALT OR KOSHER SALT

$1/4$ TEASPOON FRESHLY GROUND PEPPER

In a medium bowl whisk together all ingredients. Makes about $1^1/_2$ cups, or enough for 2 to 3 pounds fish, seafood, poultry, or pork.

Peppered Greek Marinade

$2/3$ CUP EXTRA VIRGIN OLIVE OIL

JUICE AND GRATED ZEST OF 1 LEMON

$1/4$ CUP DRY WHITE WINE

1 TABLESPOONS MINCED FRESH GARLIC

2 TEASPOONS DRIED OREGANO (PREFERABLY GREEK OR TURKISH)

1 BAY LEAF

1 TEASPOON COARSE SEA SALT OR KOSHER SALT

$1/2$ TEASPOON FRESHLY GROUND PEPPER

1 TEASPOON ALEPPO PEPPER FLAKES (OPTIONAL)

In a medium bowl whisk together all ingredients. Makes about $1^1/_4$ cups, or enough for 2 pounds fish, seafood, poultry, pork, beef, or lamb.

CYPRESS-STYLE MARINADE

1 RECIPE PEPPERED GREEK MARINADE
$^1/_4$ CUP JUICE AND 1 TEASPOON ZEST FROM
    1 ORANGE

In a medium bowl whisk together all ingredients. Makes about $1^1/_2$ cups, or enough for 2 pounds fish, seafood, poultry, pork, beef, or lamb.

TRIED & TRUE

- Cypress Swordfish with Greek Salsa (page 165)
- Sicilian Swordfish with Caponata (page 165)
- Swordfish Souvlaki with Fennel & Sun-Dried Tomato Tzatziki (page 166)
- Lamb Souvlaki with Fennel & Sun-Dried Tomato Tzatziki (page 216)

SOMETHING NEW

- Marinate chicken breast or thigh cubes in Peppered Greek Marinade. Sauté and serve with Greek Salsa (page 22) or Cucumber-Fennel Tzatziki (page 76) as a pita bread filling.
- Marinate portabella mushrooms, eggplant slices, and zucchini halves in Rosemary-Lemon Marinade for 30 to 60 minutes before grilling.

Balsamic Marinade

$^1/_2$ CUP BALSAMIC VINEGAR
$^1/_2$ CUP EXTRA VIRGIN OLIVE OIL
$^1/_2$ CUP MINCED SHALLOTS
2 TABLESPOONS MINCED FRESH ROSEMARY

1 TABLESPOON MINCED FRESH THYME
$^1/_2$ TEASPOON COARSE SEA SALT OR KOSHER SALT
$^1/_2$ TEASPOON FRESHLY GROUND PEPPER

In a medium bowl whisk together all ingredients. Makes about 1$^1/_2$ cups.

Red Wine–Balsamic Marinade

1 RECIPE BALSAMIC MARINADE
$^3/_4$ CUP DRY RED WINE

In a medium bowl whisk together all ingredients. Makes about 2$^1/_4$ cups.

Basil–Balsamic Marinade

1 RECIPE BALSAMIC MARINADE *MADE WITHOUT ROSEMARY*
$^1/_4$ CUP CHOPPED FRESH BASIL

In a medium bowl whisk together all ingredients. Makes about 1$^3/_4$ cups.

Orange–Balsamic Marinade

1 RECIPE BALSAMIC MARINADE
$^1/_2$ CUP FRESH ORANGE JUICE
1 TEASPOON GRATED ORANGE ZEST

In a medium bowl whisk together all ingredients. Makes about 2 cups.

Notes

These marinades add a delicious depth of flavor to beef, lamb, and pork tenderloin. 1 cup of marinade is enough for 2 pounds of meat.

Tried & True

- Pan Roasted Sirloin with Vegetable Relish & Tomato-Basil Butter (page 202)
- Basil Balsamic Sirloin with Aioli (page 203)
- Sicilian Sirloin (page 203)

Something New

- Marinate chicken thigh chunks in Basil-Balsamic Marinade for 2 hours. Sauté in olive oil and toss with pasta, Red Wine Marinara (page 100), and your choice of sautéed or roasted vegetables.
- Enhance the flavor of steaks with a quick 1-hour bath in Balsamic Marinade prior to grilling.

MEDITERRANEAN RED WINE MARINADE

1 CUP DRY RED WINE
2 TABLESPOONS EXTRA VIRGIN OLIVE OIL
$1/4$ CUP BALSAMIC VINEGAR
$1/4$ CUP MINCED SHALLOTS
1 TABLESPOON MINCED FRESH GARLIC
1 TABLESPOON MINCED FRESH MINT
$1^1/2$ TABLESPOONS MINCED FRESH OREGANO

1 BAY LEAF (TURKISH)
5 JUNIPER BERRIES, LIGHTLY CRUSHED
$1/2$ TEASPOON MUSTARD SEED
$1/2$ TEASPOON COARSE SEA SALT OR KOSHER SALT
$1/2$ TEASPOON FRESHLY GROUND PEPPER

In a medium bowl whisk together all ingredients. Makes about $1^3/4$ cups.

RED WINE-FENNEL MARINADE

1 RECIPE MEDITERRANEAN RED WINE MARINADE *MADE WITHOUT MINT, OREGANO, AND MUSTARD SEED*

2 TABLESPOONS MINCED FRESH TARRAGON
1 TABLESPOON FENNEL SEEDS

In a medium bowl whisk together all ingredients. Makes about $1^3/4$ cups.

RED WINE-ORANGE MARINADE

1 RECIPE MEDITERRANEAN RED WINE MARINADE *MADE WITHOUT MINT AND OREGANO*
$3/4$ CUP FRESH ORANGE JUICE

1 TEASPOON GRATED ORANGE ZEST
1 TABLESPOON MINCED FRESH THYME

In a medium bowl whisk together all ingredients. Makes about $2^1/2$ cups.

Scarborough Fair Marinade

1½ CUPS DRY RED WINE

½ CUP MINCED SHALLOTS

¼ CUP EXTRA VIRGIN OLIVE OIL

1 TABLESPOON MINCED FRESH GARLIC

1½ TABLESPOONS EACH: MINCED FRESH PARSLEY, SAGE, ROSEMARY AND THYME

1 TEASPOON MUSTARD SEED

1 TEASPOON COARSE SEA SALT OR KOSHER SALT

1 TEASPOON FRESHLY GROUND PEPPER

In a medium bowl whisk together all ingredients. Makes about 2¼ cups.

Notes

These marinades are delicious with red meat and wild game. 1 cup marinade is enough for about 2 pounds of meat.

Tried & True

- Cranberry-Port Sauce (page 92)
- Orange Infused Pork Tenderloin with Cranberry-Port Sauce (page 187)
- Scarborough Sirloin with Wild Mushrooms & Onion Jam (page 203)
- Orange Infused Lamb Chops with Cranberry-Port Sauce (page 215)
- Mediterranean Lamb Chops with Fennel & Sun-Dried Tomato Tzatziki (page 77)
- Mediterranean Lamb Roast with Greek Salsa (page 219)

Something New

- Try Mediterranean Red Wine Marinade on a venison roast. Marinate for 8 to 12 hours.
- Marinate lamb chops in Red Wine-Fennel Marinade, grill or broil, and serve drizzled with Lemon-Tarragon Aioli (page 46)
- Scarborough Fair Marinade is great for beef roasts. Marinate for 8 to 12 hours.

Mustard-Sage Marinade

$^1/_2$ CUP CHOPPED SWEET ONION

$^1/_4$ CUP EXTRA VIRGIN OLIVE OIL

3 TABLESPOONS CHOPPED FRESH SAGE

$2^1/_2$ TABLESPOONS CHOPPED ITALIAN PARSLEY

2 TABLESPOONS CHOPPED FRESH LEMON THYME OR THYME LEAVES

2 TABLESPOONS DIJON MUSTARD

2 TABLESPOONS GRAINY DIJON MUSTARD

2 TABLESPOONS FRESH LEMON JUICE

1 TABLESPOON HONEY

1 TABLESPOON WHITE WINE WORCESTERSHIRE

2 TEASPOONS CHOPPED FRESH GARLIC

1 TEASPOON GROUND FENNEL SEED

1 TEASPOON COARSE SEA SALT OR KOSHER SALT

$^1/_2$ TEASPOON FRESHLY GROUND PEPPER

In a blender or food processor combine all ingredients and purée. Makes about $1^1/_2$ cups, or enough for 3 pounds of fish, poultry, or pork or 1 whole chicken.

Notes

Why not whip up a double batch of this tasty marinade and freeze half? Pour into a ziplock freezer bag, squeeze out the air, and freeze for up to 3 months.

Tried & True

- Mustard-Sage Grilled Salmon (page 155)

Something New

- Rub the marinade on a whole chicken and allow to marinate from 4 to 12 hours. Stuff the inside of the chicken with onion chunks, lemon halves, and additional parsley, sage, and thyme sprigs before roasting in the oven.
- Marinate chicken chunks, shrimp, or scallops for 2 hours. Wrap in prosciutto or bacon. Thread onto skewers and grill or broil.

Tuscan Herb Paste

2¹/₂ TABLESPOONS EXTRA VIRGIN OLIVE OIL

2 TABLESPOONS MINCED FRESH ROSEMARY

2 TABLESPOONS MINCED FRESH FLAT-LEAF PARSLEY

¹/₂ TABLESPOON MINCED FRESH SAGE

¹/₂ TABLESPOON MINCED FRESH OREGANO

¹/₂ TABLESPOON CRUSHED FENNEL SEEDS

2 TEASPOONS MINCED FRESH GARLIC

1 TEASPOON COARSE SEA SALT OR KOSHER SALT

¹/₂ TEASPOON FRESHLY GROUND PEPPER

In a small bowl or mini-processor combine all ingredients. Purée thoroughly. Makes about ¹/₂ cup.

Tuscan Herb Marinade

1 RECIPE TUSCAN HERB PASTE

¹/₄ CUP DRY WHITE WINE

2 TABLESPOONS EXTRA VIRGIN OLIVE OIL

1 TABLESPOON WHITE BALSAMIC VINEGAR OR BALSAMIC VINEGAR

In a medium bowl whisk together all ingredients. Makes about 1 cup.

Provençal Herb Paste

2 TABLESPOONS EXTRA VIRGIN OLIVE OIL

2 TABLESPOONS MINCED FRESH ROSEMARY

1¹/₂ TABLESPOONS MINCED FRESH THYME

1 TABLESPOON MINCED FRESH TARRAGON

1 TEASPOON MINCED FRESH GARLIC

¹/₂ TEASPOON CHOPPED DRIED LAVENDER BUDS

1 TEASPOON COARSE SEA SALT OR KOSHER SALT

¹/₂ TEASPOON FRESHLY GROUND PEPPER

In a small bowl or mini-processor combine all ingredients. Purée thoroughly. Makes about ¹/₂ cup.

PROVENÇAL HERB MARINADE

1   RECIPE PROVENCAL HERB PASTE
1/4 CUP DRY WHITE WINE
2   TABLESPOONS EXTRA VIRGIN OLIVE OIL

1   TABLESPOON TARRAGON VINEGAR OR WHITE WINE VINEGAR
1   TEASPOON DIJON MUSTARD

In a medium bowl whisk together all ingredients. Makes about 1 cup.

NOTES

Both pastes and marinades make enough for about 1 1/2 to 2 pounds of seafood, fish, poultry, or meat.

TRIED & TRUE

- Provençal Fish Brochettes on Roasted Ratatouille Relish (page 167)
- Tuscan Herb Beer Can Chicken (page 177)
- Provençal Pork Tenderloin with Roasted Ratatouille Relish (page 187)
- Provençal Grilled Lamb Chops with Lemon-Tarragon Aioli (page 214)
- Tuscan Herb Roasted Leg of Lamb (page 219)

SOMETHING NEW

- Marinate cubes of chicken or shrimp in Tuscan Herb Marinade for 1–2 hours before sautéeing and add to pasta dishes.
- Rub Tuscan Herb Paste on swordfish, marlin or other firm, meaty fish before grilling, broiling or roasting.
- Marinate pork tenderloin in Tuscan Herb Marinade and roast. Serve with a side of Roasted Vegetable Panzanella (page 226)
- Rub either of the pastes under the skin of chicken, turkey, or game hens before roasting.
- Marinate shrimp in Provencal Herb Marinade for 1 hour. Drain and sauté. Serve with toothpicks and a bowl of Lemon-Tarragon Aioli for dipping.

Jamaican Jerk Marinade

2 TO 4 SCOTCH BONNET OR HABANERO PEPPERS, CHOPPED

1 BUNCH SCALLIONS, CHOPPED

1 MEDIUM SWEET ONION, CHOPPED

2 TABLESPOONS FRESH THYME LEAVES

2^1/$_2$ TABLESPOONS SOY SAUCE

2 TABLESPOONS FRESH LIME JUICE

2 TABLESPOONS DARK BROWN SUGAR

1^1/$_2$ TABLESPOONS PEANUT OIL

1 TABLESPOON PICKAPEPPA SAUCE (OR WORCESTERSHIRE)

1 TABLESPOON MINCED FRESH GARLIC

1 TABLESPOON MINCED FRESH GINGER

2 TEASPOONS GROUND ALLSPICE

1^1/$_2$ TEASPOONS COARSE SEA SALT OR KOSHER SALT

^{1}/$_2$ TEASPOON CRACKED PEPPER

^{1}/$_4$ TEASPOON NUTMEG

^{1}/$_4$ TEASPOON GROUND CINNAMON

In a food processor or blender combine all ingredients and purée. Makes about 2 cups. Enough for 4 pounds of shrimp, fish, poultry, or pork.

Jamaican Jerk Spice Rub

^{1}/$_4$ CUP DARK BROWN SUGAR

3 TABLESPOONS COARSE SEA SALT OR KOSHER SALT

2 TABLESPOONS ONION POWDER

2 TABLESPOONS FREEZE-DRIED CHIVES

2 TEASPOONS DRIED THYME

2 TEASPOONS GROUND ALLSPICE

2 TEASPOONS GROUND CORIANDER

1^1/$_2$ TO 2 TEASPOONS CAYENNE

1^1/$_2$ TEASPOONS GRANULATED GARLIC OR GARLIC POWDER

1 TEASPOON CRACKED PEPPER

^{1}/$_2$ TEASPOON GROUND CINNAMON

^{1}/$_4$ TEASPOON GROUND NUTMEG

^{1}/$_4$ TEASPOON GROUND GINGER

Thoroughly combine all ingredients. Makes about 1 cup. Store airtight in your spice cabinet for up to 6 months. Use 2 tablespoons per pound on shrimp, fish, poultry, or meat.

Notes

Although the list of ingredients here is rather long, don't cheat and skip any. Each ingredient plays a part in achieving that delicious Jamaican flavor! To get a jump on things, you can make the marinade a day ahead and keep it in the fridge.

Tried & True

- Jerk Beer Can Chicken (page 177)
- Jamaican Jerk Pork Tenderloin with Mango, Papaya, & Roasted Red Pepper Salsa (page 187)
- Jerk Pork Burgers with Grilled Pineapple and Mojo Mayo (page 197)
- Jamaican Jerk Lettuce Wraps with Savory Mango-Papaya Salsa (page 207)

Something New

- Rub baby back ribs with spice rub before barbecuing.
- Marinate pork chops or chicken thighs for 2 to 4 hours. Grill, broil, or pan-roast. Serve with any of the fruit salsas on pages 66–71 if desired.
- Rub chicken breasts with spice rub. Grill and serve with grilled red onion slices, toasted onion buns, and Mojo Mayo for tasty Caribbean-style sandwiches.

Southwest Spice Rub

$^1/_4$ CUP DARK BROWN SUGAR

3 TABLESPOONS COARSE SEA SALT OR KOSHER SALT

2 TABLESPOONS HUNGARIAN SWEET PAPRIKA

2 TABLESPOONS ANCHO CHILE POWDER

1 TABLESPOON CHIPOTLE CHILE POWDER

1 TABLESPOON GROUND CORIANDER

$1^1/_2$ TABLESPOONS GROUND CUMIN

1 TABLESPOON GRANULATED GARLIC OR GARLIC POWDER

1 TABLESPOON ONION POWDER

2 TEASPOONS DRIED OREGANO (PREFERABLY MEXICAN)

1 TABLESPOON FRESHLY GROUND PEPPER

2 TEASPOONS DRY MUSTARD

1 TEASPOON GROUND SAGE (OPTIONAL)

1 TEASPOON DRIED THYME

$^1/_2$ TEASPOON GROUND ALLSPICE

In a medium bowl thoroughly combine all ingredients. Makes about $1^1/_4$ cups. Store airtight in your spice cabinet for up to 6 months. Use 2 tablespoons per pound on fish, poultry, or meat.

Cajun-Creole Spice Rub

$^1/_4$ CUP SWEET HUNGARIAN PAPRIKA

2 TABLESPOONS COARSE SEA SALT OR KOSHER SALT

2 TABLESPOONS GRANULATED GARLIC OR GARLIC POWDER

2 TABLESPOONS ONION POWDER

$1^1/_2$ TABLESPOONS SUGAR

1 TABLESPOON CELERY SALT

1 TABLESPOON DRIED THYME

1 TABLESPOON FRESHLY GROUND PEPPER

2 TEASPOONS CAYENNE

2 TEASPOONS DRIED OREGANO

1 TEASPOON GROUND FENNEL

$^1/_4$ TEASPOON GROUND BAY LEAF

In a medium bowl thoroughly combine all ingredients. Makes about 1 cup. Store airtight in your spice cabinet for up to 6 months. Use 2 tablespoons per pound on shrimp, fish, poultry, or meat.

Tried & True

- Cajun Chicken & Andouille Skewers with Remoulade (page 137)
- Chimichurri Chicken Skewers (page 137)
- Southwest Grilled Salmon with Cilantro-Lime Butter (page 155)
- Bourbon Street Chicken with Sweet Corn Remoulade (page 173)
- Cajun Chicken & Sweet Potatoes (page 174)
- Biff's Beer Can Chicken (page 176)
- Southwest Beer Can Chicken (page 177)
- Jambalaya Burgers with Roasted Red Pepper Remoulade (page 196)
- Argentinean Flank Steak with Chimichurri Sauce (page 204)
- Southwest Spiced Flank Steak with Pancetta-Corn Salsa (page 205)
- Cajun Spiced Flank Steak with Sweet Corn Remoulade (page 205)
- Chile-Fired Burgers with Chimichurri (page 213)
- Southwest-Spiced Oven Roasted Corn (page 235)

Something New

- Both rubs are perfect for adding regional flair to grilled or pan-seared fish, steaks, chicken, pork chops, and more.
- Toss chicken or beef strips with Southwest Spice Rub and sauté for fajitas, or add to ground beef or ground turkey for tacos.
- Rub ears of corn with olive oil, then sprinkle with either rub and grill until softened and lightly browned.

ANCHO-CINNAMON SPICE RUB

2 TEASPOONS GROUND CINNAMON
2 TEASPOONS ANCHO CHILE POWDER

1 TEASPOON COARSE SEA SALT OR KOSHER SALT
$^1/_2$ TEASPOON FRESHLY GROUND PEPPER

In a small bowl thoroughly combine all ingredients. Makes enough for $1^1/_2$ pounds shrimp, fish, poultry, or meat.

CARIBBEAN RUB

$1^1/_2$ TEASPOONS GROUND ALLSPICE
$1^1/_2$ TEASPOONS DRIED THYME
1 TEASPOON COURSE SEA SALT OR KOSHER SALT

$^1/_2$ TEASPOON GROUND CORIANDER
$^1/_2$ TEASPOON FRESHLY GROUND PEPPER
$^1/_4$ TEASPOON CAYENNE
$^1/_8$ TEASPOON GROUND CLOVES

In a small bowl thoroughly combine all ingredients. Makes enough for $1^1/_2$ pounds shrimp, fish, poultry, or meat.

CHINESE 5-SPICE RUB

$1^1/_2$ TEASPOONS CHINESE 5-SPICE POWDER
$1^1/_2$ TEASPOONS DRIED BASIL
1 TEASPOON COARSE SEA SALT OR KOSHER SALT

$^1/_2$ TEASPOON FRESHLY GROUND PEPPER
$^1/_4$ TEASPOON GROUND CARDAMOM

In a small bowl thoroughly combine all ingredients. Makes enough for $1^1/_2$ pounds shrimp, fish, poultry, or meat.

CURRY-MASALA RUB

2	TABLESPOONS SWEET CURRY POWDER	1	TABLESPOON FRESHLY GROUND PEPPER
2	TABLESPOONS GARAM MASALA	1	TABLESPOON DRIED MINT
2	TABLESPOONS COARSE SEA SALT OR KOSHER SALT	1	TEASPOON GROUND CAYENNE PEPPER

In a small bowl thoroughly combine all ingredients. Makes $1/2$ cup. Use 1 tablespoon per pound on shrimp, fish, poultry, or meat.

NOTES

Rubs can be stored, airtight, in your spice cabinet for up to 6 months.

TRIED & TRUE

- 5-Spice Shrimp Skewers with Asian Maple-Mustard Glaze (page 131)
- Caribbean Shrimp Skewers (page 131)
- Ancho-Spiced Salmon with Cherry-Port Sauce (page 151)
- Masala-Spiced Sea Bass with Pineapple-Coconut Raita (page 163)
- Ancho-Cinnamon Flank Steak with Cherry-Port Sauce (page 205)

SOMETHING NEW

- Add Ancho-Cinnamon spice rub to cubed or ground beef when making chili.
- Toss thin slices of pork or beef tenderloin with Chinese 5-Spice Rub and add to stir-fried vegetables or fried rice.
- Cut winter squash (such as butternut) into 1-inch chunks and toss with a little olive oil and Curry-Masala Rub or Chinese 5-Spice Rub and roast in a 400° oven for 25 to 30 minutes.
- Rub pork chops or chicken breasts with Caribbean Rub and grill or pan-roast. Serve with any of the fruit salsas on pages 66–71 if desired.

SAVORY HERB RUB

2	TABLESPOONS COARSE SEA SALT OR KOSHER SALT	4	TEASPOONS FRESHLY GROUND PEPPER
4	TEASPOONS DRIED OREGANO	2	TEASPOONS GROUND CORIANDER
4	TEASPOONS DRIED ROSEMARY	2	TEASPOONS GROUND FENNEL SEED
4	TEASPOONS DRIED BASIL	2	TEASPOONS ONION POWDER
4	TEASPOONS GRANULATED GARLIC OR GARLIC POWDER	2	TEASPOONS DRIED THYME
		1	TEASPOON GROUND SAGE

In a small bowl thoroughly combine all ingredients. Makes about 3/4 cup.

MEDITERRANEAN SEED CRUST

1	TABLESPOON LIGHTLY CRUSHED CORIANDER SEEDS	1	TEASPOON COARSE SEA SALT OR KOSHER SALT
2	TEASPOONS LIGHTLY CRUSHED FENNEL SEEDS	$1/2$	TEASPOON FRESHLY GROUND PEPPER
1	TEASPOON LIGHTLY CRUSHED CUMIN SEEDS	$1/2$	TEASPOON DRIED OREGANO (GREEK OR TURKISH)

In a small bowl thoroughly combine all ingredients. Makes about $2^1/_2$ tablespoons, or enough for $1^1/_2$ pounds fish, poultry, or meat.

TOASTED MUSTARD SEED CRUST

1	TABLESPOON YELLOW MUSTARD SEEDS	2	TEASPOONS COARSE SEA SALT OR KOSHER SALT
1	TABLESPOON CORIANDER SEEDS	1	TEASPOON FRESHLY GROUND PEPPER
2	TEASPOONS CUMIN SEEDS	$1^1/_2$	TABLESPOONS LIGHT BROWN SUGAR (OPTIONAL)
1	TEASPOON FENNEL SEEDS		

In a small, heavy skillet over medium heat toast the mustard, coriander, cumin, and fennel seeds until fragrant, 2 to 3 minutes, shaking the pan frequently. Remove to a plate and cool. Transfer the seeds to a spice grinder or clean coffee grinder and coarsely grind. Add salt, pepper, and sugar and pulse to combine. Makes about $1/3$ cup, or enough for 3 pounds fish, poultry, or meat.

NOTES

Savory Herb Rub is a terrific, versatile rub to keep on hand. Store airtight in your spice cabinet for up to 1 year. Use 2 tablespoons per pound on meaty fish, poultry, pork, veal, beef, or lamb.

TRIED & TRUE

- Roasted Red Pepper & Garlic Corn Salsa (page 61)
- Mustard Seed Salmon with Lemon-Dill Aioli (page 157)
- Seed Crusted Salmon with Orange Romesco Sauce (page 151)
- Seed Crusted Salmon with Sautéed Mushroom Vinaigrette (page 151)
- Mediterranean Seed Crusted Tuna with Romesco Mayo (page 159)
- Seed Crusted Pork Tenderloin with Orange Romesco Sauce (page 188)
- Herb Crusted Pork Tenderloin with Mushroom & Onion Sauce (page 189)
- Herb Crusted Pork Tenderloin with Roasted Garlic, Red Wine, & Pepper Sauce (page 189)

SOMETHING NEW

- Toss red potato chunks or wedges with olive oil and Savory Herb Rub or Mediterranean Seed Crust and oven-roast at 425° for 30 minutes or until browned. Add sweet onion or fennel wedges if desired.
- Try either of the seed crusts on pan-roasted chicken breasts to really jazz up the flavor of an easy weeknight standby.
- Cut winter squash (such as butternut) into 1-inch chunks and toss with a little olive oil and Toasted Mustard Seed Crust and oven-roast at 400° for 25 to 30 minutes or until lightly browned.
- Toss a little Toasted Mustard Seed Crust with cooked rice or couscous for a savory side dish. Add minced scallions, cilantro, lemon zest, and/or Italian parsley if desired.

FLAVORED MAYONNAISE AND COMPOUND BUTTER

The recipes in this section are used in myriad ways throughout the book. Flavored mayo makes a terrific topping for burgers, dip for appetizers, or sauce for meats. Aioli, the classic garlic-flavored mayonnaise from France, takes on many versions here. Although purists would claim that aioli must be made from scratch, I find that using a good quality mayonnaise, such as Hellmann's, is equally delicious and eliminates the worry that comes from using raw eggs.

Compound butters make an easy and delicious topping for meats and can be mixed into potatoes, pasta, and vegetables for a quick flavor boost. Freeze compound butters, tightly wrapped in plastic, and you'll always have some on hand to jazz up your weeknight meals!

Wasabi Mayo

$^1/_2$ CUP MAYONNAISE	1 TABLESPOON ASIAN SESAME OIL
1 TABLESPOON WASABI PASTE	1 TEASPOON SUGAR

In a small bowl thoroughly whisk together all ingredients. Makes about $^2/_3$ cup.

Oriental Orange Mayo

$^1/_2$ TABLESPOONS PEANUT OIL	3 TABLESPOONS SOY SAUCE
$^1/_4$ CUP MINCED SCALLIONS (WHITE AND LIGHT GREEN PARTS ONLY)	2 TABLESPOONS RICE VINEGAR
1 TABLESPOON MINCED FRESH GINGER	1 TABLESPOON LIGHT BROWN SUGAR
1 TEASPOON MINCED FRESH GARLIC	2 WHOLE STAR ANISE
4 TABLESPOONS JUICE PLUS 2 TEASPOONS GRATED ZEST FROM 1 ORANGE	$^1/_2$ CUP MAYONNAISE

In a small saucepan heat the peanut oil over medium high heat. Add the scallions, ginger, and garlic, and sauté for 2 minutes. Add 2 tablespoons orange juice, the soy sauce, rice vinegar, brown sugar, and star anise. Bring to a boil, stirring to dissolve the sugar. Reduce heat and simmer for 10 minutes. Cool slightly, discard the star anise, and remove the mixture to a blender or mini-processor. Add the remaining 2 tablespoons orange juice, orange zest, and mayonnaise and purée. Makes about $1^1/_4$ cups.

NOTES

Mayos will keep, covered, in the refrigerator for up to 2 days.

TRIED & TRUE

- Sesame Seared Tuna with Oriental Orange Mayo (page 158)
- Sesame Seared Tuna with Wasabi Mayo and Ponzu Dipping Sauce (page 159)
- Sushi Burgers with Wasabi Mayo (page 161)

SOMETHING NEW

- Mix Oriental Orange Mayo into chicken salad, along with chopped water chestnuts and red pepper; use for sandwiches or serve in pineapple or papaya halves.
- Drizzle Oriental Orange Mayo over grilled or roasted asparagus or steamed sugar snap peas.
- Use either mayo as a dipping sauce for Teriyaki-marinated grilled shrimp or scallops.
- Coat skinless salmon cubes in sesame seeds and roast in a 450° oven until cooked through; serve with toothpicks, accompanied by either or both of the mayos for dipping.

Mojo Mayo

1 CUP MAYONNAISE

2 TABLESPOONS FRESH ORANGE JUICE

1 TEASPOON GRATED ORANGE ZEST

1 TABLESPOON FRESH LIME JUICE
GRATED ZEST FROM 1 LIME

1 MEDIUM SHALLOT, CHOPPED

2 TABLESPOONS CHOPPED FRESH CILANTRO

2 TEASPOONS CHOPPED CHIPOTLE CHILES IN ADOBO

1 TEASPOON CHOPPED FRESH GARLIC
SEA SALT AND FRESHLY GROUND PEPPER
NOTE: 1½ TABLESPOONS FROZEN, THAWED ORANGE JUICE CONCENTRATE MAY BE SUBSTITUTED FOR THE FRESH ORANGE JUICE AND ORANGE ZEST IF DESIRED

In a blender or mini-processor combine the mayonnaise, orange juice, orange zest, lime juice, lime zest, shallot, cilantro, chiles, and garlic. Purée. Season to taste with salt and pepper. Makes about 1½ cups.

Romesco Mayo

½ CUP MAYONNAISE

½ CUP CHOPPED ROASTED RED PEPPERS (PAGE 9 OR STORE-BOUGHT)

¼ CUP BLANCHED, SLIVERED ALMONDS, LIGHTLY TOASTED

2 TABLESPOONS DOUBLE STRENGTH TOMATO PASTE

1½ TABLESPOONS CHOPPED SHALLOT

1½ TEASPOONS ROASTED GARLIC (PAGE 8 OR STORE-BOUGHT)

1 TEASPOON SHERRY VINEGAR

½ TEASPOONS SPANISH SMOKED PAPRIKA (PIMENTON)
SEA SALT AND FRESHLY GROUND PEPPER TO TASTE

In a blender or mini-processor combine the mayonnaise, peppers, almonds, tomato paste, shallot, garlic, vinegar, and paprika. Purée. Season to taste with salt and pepper. Makes about 1¼ cups.

NOTES

Mayos will keep, covered, in the refrigerator for up to 2 days.

TRIED & TRUE

Mediterranean Seed Crusted Tuna with Romesco Mayo (page 159)
Jerk Pork Burgers with Grilled Pineapple & Mojo Mayo (page 197)
Spanish-Spiced Pork Burgers with Romesco Mayo (page 197)

SOMETHING NEW

*   Mix Romesco Mayo with chicken cubes, chopped scallions, celery, and bell peppers for chicken salad sandwiches.
*   Spread either mayo on turkey sandwiches.
*   Mix Mojo Mayo with shredded cabbage, carrots, red bell peppers, and pineapple chunks for a Caribbean-flavored coleslaw.

LEMON-TARRAGON AIOLI

$^1/_2$ CUP MAYONNAISE

1 MEDIUM SHALLOT, CHOPPED

$1^1/_2$ TABLESPOONS FRESH LEMON JUICE

1 TEASPOON GRATED LEMON ZEST

2 TABLESPOONS CHOPPED FRESH TARRAGON

$1^1/_2$ TEASPOONS MINCED FRESH GARLIC

$1^1/_2$ TEASPOONS DIJON MUSTARD

SEA SALT AND FRESHLY GROUND PEPPER

In a blender or mini-processor combine the mayonnaise, shallot, lemon juice, lemon zest, tarragon, garlic, and mustard. Purée. Season to taste with salt and pepper. Makes about $^3/_4$ cup.

LEMON-DILL AIOLI

Replace the tarragon with $2^1/_2$–3 tablespoons chopped fresh dill and add $1^1/_2$ teaspoons grainy Dijon mustard. Proceed as above. Makes about $^3/_4$ cup.

MAKE-IT-YOUR-OWN LEMON AIOLI

Replace the tarragon with another fresh, tender herb, such as: basil, chives, chervil, flat-leaf parsley, cilantro, mint, or a combination of these.

Notes

Aiolis will keep, covered, in the refrigerator for up to 2 days.

Tried & True

- Mustard Seed Salmon with Lemon-Dill Aioli (page 157)
- Honey-Mustard Tuna Burgers (page 161)
- Provençal Grilled Lamb Chops with Lemon-Tarragon Aioli (page 214)

Something New

- Mix Lemon-Tarragon Aioli into chicken or turkey salad, along with some dried cranberries and toasted pecans for sandwiches.
- Use either aioli as a dressing for potato salad.
- Drizzle either aioli over steamed asparagus or broccoli spears.
- Serve Lemon-Dill Aioli with smoked salmon as part of a brunch or hors d'oeuvres buffet.

Roasted Garlic & Red Pepper Aioli

$^1/_2$ CUP MAYONNAISE

$^1/_2$ CUP CHOPPED ROASTED RED PEPPERS (PAGE 9 OR STORE-BOUGHT)

1 MEDIUM SHALLOT, CHOPPED

1 TABLESPOON ROASTED GARLIC (PAGE 8 OR STORE-BOUGHT)

$^1/_2$ TABLESPOONS WORCESTERSHIRE SAUCE

A FEW DASHES HOT SAUCE (OPTIONAL)

SEA SALT AND FRESHLY GROUND PEPPER

In a blender or mini-processor combine the mayonnaise, peppers, shallot, garlic, and Worcestershire sauce. Purée. Season to taste with hot sauce, if desire, and salt and pepper. Makes about $1^1/_4$ cups.

Sun-Dried Tomato & Basil Aioli

$^1/_2$ CUP MAYONNAISE

$^1/_4$ CUP OIL PACKED SUN-DRIED TOMATOES, DRAINED AND CHOPPED

1 TABLESPOON OIL RESERVED FROM SUN-DRIED TOMATOES

1 MEDIUM SHALLOT, CHOPPED

1 TABLESPOON DOUBLE CONCENTRATED TOMATO PASTE

$1^1/_2$ TEASPOONS MINCED FRESH GARLIC

$^1/_4$ CUP MINCED FRESH BASIL

SEA SALT AND FRESHLY GROUND PEPPER

In a blender or mini-processor combine the mayonnaise, sun-dried tomatoes and oil, shallot, tomato paste, and garlic. Purée. Stir in the basil. Season to taste with salt and pepper. Makes about $1^1/_4$ cups.

NOTES

Both of the aiolis will keep, covered, in the refrigerator for up to 2 days.

TRIED & TRUE

- Chicken-Chorizo Skewers with Roasted Garlic & Red Pepper Aioli (page 136)
- Basil-Balsamic Sirloin with Aioli (page 203)

SOMETHING NEW

- Both of the aiolis make terrific sandwich spreads or burger toppings.
- Use Sun-Dried Tomato & Basil Aioli as a dip for crudités.
- Drizzle Sun-Dried Tomato & Basil Aioli over grilled eggplant and zucchini.

Roasted Red Pepper Remoulade

$1/2$ CUP CHOPPED ROASTED RED PEPPER (PAGE 9 OR STORE-BOUGHT), PATTED DRY

$1/2$ CUP MAYONNAISE

3 TABLESPOONS MINCED CELERY

2 TABLESPOONS MINCED ITALIAN PARSLEY

1 TABLESPOON MINCED SHALLOT

1 TABLESPOON CREOLE MUSTARD (OR OTHER SPICY MUSTARD)

1 TABLESPOON PREPARED OR CREAM-STYLE HORSERADISH

1 TABLESPOON WORCESTERSHIRE SAUCE

1 TEASPOON MINCED FRESH GARLIC

$1/2$ TEASPOON LOUISIANA-STYLE HOT SAUCE

In a mini-processor or blender combine all ingredients and purée to a slightly chunky sauce. Refrigerate, covered, up to 24 hours. Makes about $1^1/4$ cups.

Sweet Corn Remoulade

1 TABLESPOON BUTTER

2 CUPS FRESH CORN KERNELS

$1/2$ CUP MAYONNAISE

$1/3$ CUP RED BELL PEPPER

$1/4$ CUP CHOPPED CELERY

2 TABLESPOONS MINCED ITALIAN PARSLEY

1 TABLESPOON MINCED SHALLOT

1 TABLESPOON WORCESTERSHIRE SAUCE

1 TABLESPOON CREOLE MUSTARD (OR OTHER SPICY MUSTARD)

1 TABLESPOON PREPARED OR CREAM-STYLE HORSERADISH

1 TEASPOON MINCED FRESH GARLIC

$1/2$ TEASPOON LOUISIANA-STYLE HOT SAUCE

In a medium nonstick skillet heat the butter over medium-high heat. Add the corn and sauté for 4 minutes. Remove to a medium bowl.

In a blender or mini-processor combine the mayonnaise, bell pepper, celery, parsley, shallot, Worcestershire sauce, mustard, horseradish, garlic, and hot sauce. Purée to a slightly chunky sauce. Add to the corn and stir to combine. Refrigerate if not using within one hour, up to 24 hours. Serve at room temperature. Makes about 3 cups.

TRIED & TRUE

- Cajun Chicken & Andouille Skewers with Remoulade (page 137)
- Bourbon Street Chicken with Sweet Corn Remoulade (page 173)
- Jambalaya Burgers with Roasted Red Pepper Remoulade (page 196)
- Cajun Spiced Flank Steak with Sweet Corn Remoulade (page 205)

SOMETHING NEW

- Add a Cajun flair to simple pan-roasted pork chops or chicken breasts with Roasted Red Pepper Remoulade.
- Serve Sweet Corn Remoulade as a bed for pecan-crusted catfish fillets or grilled salmon dusted with Cajun-Creole Spice Rub (page 34)

Smoked Paprika & Roasted Garlic Butter

1   STICK UNSALTED BUTTER, SOFTENED
1¹/₂ TABLESPOONS ROASTED GARLIC (PAGE 8 OR
    STORE-BOUGHT)
2   TEASPOONS WHITE WINE WORCESTERSHIRE
    SAUCE

1   TEASPOON SMOKED PAPRIKA
    SEA SALT AND FRESHLY GROUND PEPPER TO
    TASTE

In a small bowl thoroughly mix all ingredients. Scrape out onto a sheet of plastic wrap and form the mixture into a log, wrapping tightly. Refrigerate until firm, at least 1 hour, or up to 3 days. Can be frozen, tightly wrapped, for up to 4 months.

Smoky Chipotle Butter

1   STICK UNSALTED BUTTER, SOFTENED
2   TABLESPOONS MINCED SHALLOTS
1¹/₂ TABLESPOONS SEEDED, MINCED CHIPOTLE
    CHILES IN ADOBO SAUCE
1   TABLESPOON FRESH LIME JUICE

2   TEASPOONS ROASTED GARLIC (PAGE 8 OR
    STORE-BOUGHT)
¹/₄ TEASPOON SMOKED PAPRIKA (OPTIONAL)
    SEA SALT AND FRESHLY GROUND PEPPER TO
    TASTE

In a small bowl thoroughly mix all ingredients. Scrape out onto a sheet of plastic wrap and form the mixture into a log, wrapping tightly. Refrigerate until firm, at least 1 hour, or up to 3 days. Can be frozen, tightly wrapped, for up to 4 months.

Tried & True

- Grilled Rib-Eyes with Smoked Paprika & Roasted Garlic Butter (page 201)
- Bourbon-Molasses Rib-Eyes with Smoky Chipotle Butter (page 201)
- Southwest Spiced Flank Steak with Pancetta-Corn Salsa (page 205)
- Twice-Baked Sweet Potatoes with Smoky Chipotle Butter (page 233)

Something New

- Brush either butter over corn on the cob.
- Stuff a slice of either butter in the middle of hamburgers before grilling or broiling.
- Place a slice of either butter atop pan-roasted salmon fillets or pork chops.
- Brush either butter over grilled shrimp or scallop skewers.

Gorgonzola–Walnut Butter

1   stick unsalted butter, softened
1/3 cup crumbled Gorgonzola* cheese
1/4 cup lightly toasted, chopped walnuts
1/2 teaspoons Hungarian sweet paprika

1/2 teaspoon freshly ground pepper
1/4 teaspoon sea salt
*Another blue cheese may be substituted.

In a small bowl thoroughly mix all ingredients. Scrape out onto a sheet of plastic wrap and form the mixture into a log, wrapping tightly. Refrigerate until firm, at least 1 hour or up to 3 days. Can be frozen, tightly wrapped, for up to 4 months.

Tomato–Basil Butter

1   stick unsalted butter, softened
4   sundried tomato halves, packed in oil, drained, minced
3   tablespoons minced fresh basil
1   tablespoon double concentrated tomato paste (or 2 tablespoons regular tomato paste)

1/2 teaspoon roasted garlic (page 8 or store-bought)
Sea salt and freshly ground pepper to taste

In a small bowl thoroughly mix all ingredients. Scrape out onto a sheet of plastic wrap and form the mixture into a log, wrapping tightly. Refrigerate until firm, at least 1 hour, or up to 3 days. Can be frozen, tightly wrapped, for up to 4 months.

Tried & True

- Rosemary Grilled Rib-Eyes with Gorgonzola-Walnut Butter (page 200)
- Pan-Roasted Sirloin with Vegetable Relish & Tomato-Basil Butter (page 202)

Something New

- Stuff a slice of either butter into beef or turkey burgers before grilling or broiling.
- Try Gorgonzola-Walnut Butter atop salmon fillets and Tomato-Basil Butter atop swordfish fillets.
- Toss either butter with orzo or rice.
- Toss either butter with sautéed green beans.
- Stuff Tomato-Basil Butter into the center of chicken breasts before pan-roasting.

Cilantro-Lime Butter

1 STICK UNSALTED BUTTER, SOFTENED

1/4 CUP MINCED FRESH CILANTRO

2 TABLESPOONS MINCED SCALLION

1 MINCED RED JALAPEÑO PEPPER (OR OTHER RED CHILE)

1 TABLESPOON FRESH LIME JUICE

1/2 TEASPOON GRATED LIME ZEST

1/2 TEASPOON GROUND CUMIN

SEA SALT AND FRESHLY GROUND PEPPER TO TASTE

In a small bowl thoroughly mix all ingredients. Scrape out onto a sheet of plastic wrap and form mixture into a log, wrapping tightly. Refrigerate until firm, at least 1 hour, or up to 3 days. Can be frozen for up to 4 months.

Shallot-Herb Butter

1 STICK UNSALTED BUTTER, SOFTENED

2 TABLESPOONS MINCED SHALLOT

1/2 TABLESPOON MINCED FRESH GARLIC

1 1/2 TABLESPOONS MINCED FRESH CHIVES

1 1/2 TABLESPOONS MINCED ITALIAN PARSLEY

1/2 TEASPOON MINCED LEMON ZEST

SEA SALT AND FRESHLY GROUND PEPPER TO TASTE

In a small sauté pan heat 1/2 tablespoon butter over medium heat. Add shallots and garlic and sauté for 2 minutes. Remove to a small bowl and cool completely. Add remaining ingredients and mix well. Use as is or cover with plastic wrap and refrigerate for up to 3 days. This butter can also be formed into a log, as above, and frozen for up to 4 months.

Tried and True

- Southwest Grilled Salmon with Cilantro-Lime Butter (page 155)
- Southwest Spiced Flank Steak with Pancetta-Corn Salsa (page 205)
- Mixed Green Salads (page 224)
- Twice-Baked Sweet Potatoes with Cilantro-Lime Butter (page 233)

Something New

- Softened Shallot-Herb Butter makes a great spread for bread . . . perfect for dinner parties.
- Try either butter on corn on the cob or grilled vegetables.
- Try either butter on sautéed zucchini and summer squash.
- Mix Shallot-Herb Butter into mashed potatoes.
- Try either butter atop grilled salmon, sea bass or other fish.

SALSAS, CHUTNEYS, RELISHES, AND OTHER TOPPINGS

This is my favorite section of the book. An intensely flavored salsa or relish can take a simple piece of fish, a plain chicken breast, or a burger from ordinary to sublime!

You'll find recipes in this section that incorporate flavors and ingredients from the world over. A well stocked pantry will ensure that you only need to pick up a few fresh ingredients to make any of the recipes in this section.

Feeling like Asian food tonight? Stir up a batch of Cucumber-Pineapple Salsa to serve with grilled fish, chicken breasts or pork chops. Sitting on a bag of ripe mangoes? Try that same fish, chicken, or pork with any of the mango salsas on pages 70–71.

While most of the fresh salsas taste best shortly after they're made, go ahead and make them early in the day if you're entertaining. Many of the chutneys and other relishes can be made well in advance.

Pancetta-Corn Salsa

2	TABLESPOONS OLIVE OIL	1	TEASPOON MINCED FRESH GARLIC
2	CUPS FRESH CORN KERNELS (ABOUT 2 LARGE EARS)	1/2	TEASPOON DRIED OREGANO (MEXICAN PREFERRED)
3/4	CUP DICED RED BELL PEPPER	2	TABLESPOONS MINCED FRESH CILANTRO
2	OUNCES PANCETTA, CHOPPED	1	TABLESPOON FRESH LIME JUICE
1	BUNCH SCALLIONS, MINCED, WHITE AND HALF OF GREEN PARTS		SEA SALT AND FRESHLY GROUND PEPPER
1	TO 2 JALAPEÑO PEPPERS, SEEDED AND MINCED		

In a large skillet heat the olive oil over medium-high heat. Add the corn, red pepper, and pancetta, and sauté for 10 minutes or until vegetables and pancetta are beginning to brown. Add the scallions, jalapeños, garlic, and oregano, and sauté for 2 minutes. Remove from heat. Stir in the cilantro and lime juice. Season to taste with salt and pepper. Makes about 2$\frac{1}{2}$ cups.

This sweet, savory, summery salsa has tons of uses! Try some of mine . . . then come up with some of your own!

Smoky Southwestern Corn Salsa

Add 4 teaspoons Southwestern Spice Rub (page 34) to Pancetta-Corn Salsa halfway through sautéeing the corn mixture. Continue as directed above.

Roasted Red Pepper & Garlic Corn Salsa

2   TABLESPOONS OLIVE OIL
2   CUPS FRESH CORN KERNELS (ABOUT 2 LARGE EARS)*
1/2 CUP CHOPPED SWEET ONION
2   OUNCES CHOPPED PANCETTA OR THICK-CUT BACON
1/2 CUP CHOPPED ROASTED RED PEPPERS (PAGE 9 OR STORE-BOUGHT)
1   TABLESPOON ROASTED GARLIC (PAGE 8 OR STORE-BOUGHT)
2   TEASPOONS TOASTED MUSTARD SEED CRUST (PAGE 38; OPTIONAL)
2   TABLESPOONS CHOPPED FRESH BASIL
2   TEASPOONS SHERRY VINEGAR
    SEA SALT AND FRESHLY GROUND PEPPER TO TASTE

In a large skillet heat the olive oil over medium-high heat. Add the corn, onion, and pancetta, and sauté for 8 minutes. Mix in the red peppers, garlic, and seed mixture, and sauté for 5 minutes. Remove from heat. Stir in the basil and vinegar. Season to taste with salt and pepper. Makes about 3 cups.

Note: Fresh corn kernels may be substituted with frozen, thawed corn.

Tried & True

- Gruyère Stuffed Salmon Burgers with Corn Salsa (page 153)
- Poblano Stuffed Chicken with Pancetta-Corn Salsa (page 170)
- Southwest Spiced Flank Steak with Pancetta-Corn Salsa (page 205)
- Southwest Corn Smashed Potatoes (page 231)
- Green Beans with Bacon & Corn (page 239)

Something New

- All of the corn salsas are great on grilled steak, chicken, pork chops, and salmon.
- Serve any of the salsas with tortilla chips.
- Toss any of the salsas with stir-fried zucchini, summer squash, or sugar snap peas.
- Toss any of the salsas with couscous or orzo for a delicious and colorful side dish.

Salsa Fresca

3 cups seeded, chopped ripe tomatoes
1 cup minced red onion or sweet onion
1 cup minced mixed chile peppers (red and green jalapeño peppers, serranos, anaheims, etc.)
³/₄ cup minced fresh cilantro
Juice and grated zest from 1 lime
2 tablespoons extra virgin olive oil
1 tablespoon minced fresh garlic

1 tablespoon sherry vinegar or raspberry vinegar (optional)
1¹/₂ teaspoons ground cumin
1 teaspoon dried oregano (Mexican preferred)
Sea salt and freshly ground pepper to taste
Habanero hot sauce to taste (optional)

In a large bowl mix together all ingredients. Let rest at room temperature for 30 minutes or refrigerate for up to 2 hours. Strain out some of the liquid before serving if desired. Makes about 5 cups.

Tomato-Mango Salsa

1 recipe Salsa Fresca
2 ripe mangos, chopped

In a large bowl mix together all ingredients. Let rest at room temperature for 30 minutes or refrigerate for up to 2 hours. Strain out some of the liquid before serving if desired. Makes about 7 cups.

Guacamole

1 recipe Salsa Fresca
2 ripe avocados

Peel and chop the avocados. Add to the Salsa Fresca and lightly mash with a fork. Serve immediately. Makes about 6 cups.

Tried & True

- Guacamole Shrimp Cocktail (page 133)
- Margarita Swordfish with Tomato-Mango Salsa (page 164)
- Southwest Turkey Burgers with Guacamole (page 182)

Something New

- Spoon Salsa Fresca over sautéed vegetables such as summer squash, zucchini, or green beans.
- Toss Salsa Fresca with rice for a colorful, spicy side dish.
- Tomato-Mango Salsa is terrific served alongside grilled fish or chicken breasts.
- Any of these salsas are perfect for serving with tortilla chips, tacos, nachos, fajitas, or quesadillas.

Coconut-Corn Salsa

2 TABLESPOONS PEANUT OIL

2 CUPS FRESH CORN KERNELS (ABOUT 2 LARGE EARS)

1 MEDIUM RED BELL PEPPER, DICED

1 CUP DICED MAUI ONION, OR OTHER SWEET ONION

3 CLOVES GARLIC, MINCED

1 TABLESPOON MINCED FRESH GINGER

1 CUP CANNED COCONUT MILK (LITE OR REGULAR)

2 TABLESPOONS TERIYAKI MARINADE (PAGE 16 OR STORE-BOUGHT)

1 TABLESPOON SOY SAUCE

1 TABLESPOON ASIAN SESAME OIL

1 TABLESPOON RICE VINEGAR OR SHERRY VINEGAR

1/4 CUP MINCED FRESH CILANTRO

1/2 TO 3/4 TEASPOON ASIAN CHILE SAUCE

In a large skillet heat the peanut oil over medium-high heat. Add corn, bell pepper and onion and sauté until vegetables are tender and beginning to brown, about 12 minutes. Make a well in the center of the pan and add the garlic and ginger. Sauté for 2 additional minutes, gradually incorporating the corn mixture.

Add coconut milk and teriyaki marinade and bring to a boil. Boil until liquid is completely evaporated, about 5 minutes. Remove mixture from heat and stir in remaining ingredients. Serve warm or at room temperature. Makes about 4 cups.

Can be made up to 6 hours in advance and refrigerated. Bring to room temperature or warm slightly before serving.

Edamame Salsa

2 CUPS FRESH, SHELLED EDAMAME, OR FROZEN, THAWED

2 TABLESPOONS PEANUT OIL

2 CUPS THINLY SLICED SHIITAKE MUSHROOM CAPS

1 TABLESPOON MINCED FRESH GINGER

1 TABLESPOON MINCED FRESH GARLIC

$^1/_2$ CUP MINCED SCALLIONS

$^1/_2$ CUP CHOPPED YELLOW BELL PEPPER

$^1/_2$ CUP CHOPPED ROASTED RED PEPPER (PAGE 9 OR STORE-BOUGHT)

$^1/_2$ CUP CHICKEN BROTH

$^1/_4$ CUP CHOPPED FRESH CILANTRO

2 TABLESPOONS DRAINED AND CHOPPED PICKLED GINGER (ALSO CALLED SUSHI GINGER)

2 TABLESPOONS TOASTED SESAME SEEDS

$1^1/_2$ TABLESPOONS SOY SAUCE

1 TABLESPOON ASIAN SESAME OIL

1 TEASPOON ASIAN CHILE GARLIC SAUCE

Cook edamame in boiling salted water for 3 minutes. Drain. Rinse with cold water to halt the cooking and drain again. Heat peanut oil in a large skillet over medium heat. Add mushrooms and sauté until the liquid they release has evaporated, about 8 minutes. Make a well in the center of the pan and add the ginger and garlic. Sauté for 1 minute. Stir in the edamame, scallions and yellow pepper and sauté for 2 minutes. Add the roasted red pepper and broth and cook for 3 minutes, or until the liquid has evaporated. Remove salsa to a bowl and stir in the remaining ingredients. Serve warm or at room temperature. Makes about 4 cups.

Can be made up to 6 hours in advance and refrigerated. Bring to room temperature or warm slightly before serving.

Tried & True

- Teriyaki Grilled Sea Bass with Coconut Corn Salsa (page 163)
- Miso Grilled Sea Bass with Edamame Salsa (page 163)
- Teriyaki Sirloin with Coconut Corn Salsa (page 203)

Something New

- Mix Coconut Corn Salsa into cooked rice for a great Asian-accented side dish.
- Serve Edamame Salsa as a side dish for any Asian-flavored entrée.
- Serve Edamame Salsa in a bowl surrounded by sesame crackers or teriyaki-flavored rice crackers for scooping.

Cucumber–Pineapple Salsa

1½ cups seeded, diced cucumber
¾ cup diced fresh pineapple
4 scallions, minced, white and light green parts only
Grated zest of 1 lime
1½ tablespoons fresh lime juice
2 tablespoons seasoned rice vinegar

2 teaspoons Asian sesame oil
1½ teaspoons soy sauce
1 tablespoon toasted sesame seeds
3 tablespoons minced fresh cilantro
¾ teaspoon Asian chile garlic sauce

In a medium bowl thoroughly combine all ingredients. Refrigerate until needed, up to 2 hours. Stir well before serving and serve with a slotted spoon. Makes about 3 cups.

Maui Wowee Salsa

2 cups chopped Maui onion (or other sweet onion)
½ cup minced scallions
¼ cup drained and chopped pickled ginger (also called sushi ginger)

¼ cup chopped cilantro
2 tablespoons Asian sesame oil
1½ tablespoons soy sauce
1 tablespoon fresh lime juice

In a medium bowl thoroughly combine all ingredients. Refrigerate until needed, up to 2 hours. Makes about 3 cups.

Tried & True

- Pac-Rim Shrimp Cocktail (page 133)
- Hawaiian Tuna Burgers with Maui Wowee Salsa (page 160)
- Teriyaki Tuna Burgers with Cucumber-Pineapple Salsa (page 161)
- Thai Lemongrass Grilled Pork Tenderloin with Cucumber-Pineapple Salsa (page 186)
- Thai Coconut Lettuce Wraps with Cucumber-Pineapple Salsa (page 207)

Something New

- Serve either salsa atop teriyaki-marinated and grilled tuna, salmon, chicken, or pork chops.
- Serve Cucumber-Pineapple Salsa in a bowl surrounded by teriyaki-flavored rice crackers or sesame crackers for scooping.
- Toss Cucumber-Pineapple Salsa into cooked rice for a tasty side dish with an Asian flair.

Floribbean Grilled Salsa

2 TABLESPOONS OLIVE OIL

2 TABLESPOONS DARK RUM OR MOJO MARINADE (PAGE 20)

2 1-INCH THICK ROUND SLICES OF FRESH PINEAPPLE

1 RED BELL PEPPER, QUARTERED AND SEEDED

2 TO 3 JALAPEÑO PEPPERS, HALVED AND SEEDED

1 BUNCH SCALLIONS, TRIMMED

1 CUP DICED FRESH PAPAYA

1 ORANGE, ZEST GRATED, SEGMENTS REMOVED AND CHOPPED

1/4 CUP MINCED FRESH CILANTRO

2 TABLESPOONS FRESH LIME JUICE, PLUS MORE TO TASTE

SEA SALT AND FRESHLY GROUND PEPPER TO TASTE

HABANERO HOT SAUCE (SUCH AS MELINDA'S; OPTIONAL)

Preheat the grill to medium-high heat.

In a small bowl whisk together the olive oil and rum. Brush over the pineapple slices, peppers, and scallions.

Grill the pineapple slices, peppers, and scallions until lightly charred and slightly softened, turning and moving around the grill as needed. This will take about 4 to 8 minutes. Remove items to a cutting board as they are done.

Cut the rind off the pineapple, remove the core, and chop the flesh. Place in a large bowl. Chop the peppers and scallions and add to the pineapple. Add the papaya, orange zest, chopped orange, cilantro, and lime juice. Mix thoroughly and season to taste with salt, pepper, hot sauce, and additional lime juice if desired. Makes about 3 cups.

Notes

This salsa is also delicious without grilling the pineapple and vegetables. Omit olive oil and rum.

Tried & True

- Floribbean Shrimp Cocktail (page 133)
- Mojo Grilled Sea Bass with Floribbean Salsa (page 162)

Something New

- Serve alongside any grilled meat, poultry, fish, or seafood.
- Mix with cooked rice and black beans for a hearty side with a Caribbean flair.

Mango, Papaya & Roasted Red Pepper Salsa

3/4 CUP CHOPPED ROASTED RED PEPPER (PAGE 9 OR STORE-BOUGHT)

1/2 CUP PEELED, DICED MANGO

1/2 CUP PEELED, DICED PAPAYA

1/2 CUP MINCED RED ONION

1/4 CUP CHOPPED CILANTRO

1 TO 2 JALAPEÑO PEPPERS, SEEDED AND MINCED

2 TABLESPOONS FRESH LIME JUICE

1 TEASPOON MINCED FRESH GINGER

1/2 TEASPOON GROUND CUMIN

SEA SALT AND FRESHLY GROUND PEPPER

HABANERO HOT SAUCE (SUCH AS MELINDA'S)

In a large bowl thoroughly combine the red pepper, mango, papaya, onion, cilantro, jalapeños, lime juice, ginger, and cumin. Season to taste with salt, pepper, and hot sauce. Set aside for 30 minutes to allow flavors to blend, or refrigerate for up to 2 hours. Makes about 2 cups.

Savory Mango-Papaya Salsa

1 TABLESPOON OLIVE OIL

3/4 CUP MINCED SWEET ONION

2 TABLESPOONS SEEDED, MINCED JALAPEÑO PEPPERS

1 TEASPOON MINCED GARLIC

1 TEASPOON GROUND CUMIN

1/2 CUP PEELED, DICED MANGO

1/2 CUP PEELED, DICED PAPAYA

1 CUP QUARTERED CHERRY TOMATOES

1/2 CUP CHOPPED ROASTED RED PEPPERS (PAGE 9 OR STORE-BOUGHT)

1/4 CUP MINCED FRESH CILANTRO

2 TABLESPOONS FRESH LIME JUICE

SEA SALT AND FRESHLY GROUND PEPPER

HABANERO HOT SAUCE (SUCH AS MELINDA'S)

In a medium skillet heat the oil over medium heat and sauté the onion for 3 minutes. Add the jalapeño, garlic, and cumin, and sauté for 2 minutes. Stir in the mango, papaya, tomatoes, and red pepper, and sauté for 2 additional minutes. Remove from heat and stir in the cilantro and lime juice. Season to taste with salt, pepper, and hot sauce. Cool to room temperature or serve chilled. May be refrigerated for up to 2 hours. Makes about 2 cups.

Savory Caribbean Salsa

1	RECIPE SAVORY MANGO-PAPAYA SALSA	1	CUP DICED FRESH PINEAPPLE
$^1/_4$	TEASPOON GROUND ALLSPICE		

Follow the directions for Savory Mango-Papaya Salsa, adding the allspice along with the cumin and adding the pineapple along with the mango. Makes about 3 cups.

Tried & True

- Caribbean Shrimp Cocktail (page 132)
- Mojo Swordfish with Savory Caribbean Salsa (page 165)
- Jamaican Jerk Pork Tenderloin with Mango, Papaya & Roasted Red Pepper Salsa (page 187)
- Jamaican Jerk Lettuce Wraps with Savory Mango-Papaya Salsa (page 207)

Something New

- Mix Savory Caribbean Salsa with cubes of smoked turkey and serve in pineapple boats.
- Serve any of the salsas as a dip for tortilla chips.
- Toss Savory Mango-Papaya Salsa with sautéed chicken breast strips and serve with lettuce leaves or cilantro-flavored tortillas for wrapping.

Greek Salsa

1/4 CUP EXTRA VIRGIN OLIVE OIL (PREFERABLY GREEK)

2 TABLESPOONS RED WINE VINEGAR

3 TABLESPOONS CHOPPED ITALIAN PARSLEY

1 1/2 TABLESPOONS CHOPPED FRESH MINT

1 1/2 TEASPOONS ROASTED GARLIC (PAGE 8 OR STORE-BOUGHT) OR 3/4 TEASPOONS MINCED FRESH GARLIC

1/2 TEASPOON DRIED OREGANO (PREFERABLY GREEK OR TURKISH)

1 1/2 CUPS SEEDED, DICED CUCUMBER

1 1/2 CUPS SEEDED, DICED TOMATO

1/2 CUP DICED RED BELL PEPPER

1/3 CUP DICED RED ONION

1/3 CUP PITTED, CHOPPED KALAMATA OLIVES

1/2 CUP CRUMBLED FETA CHEESE

SEA SALT AND FRESHLY GROUND PEPPER

In a large bowl whisk together the oil, vinegar, parsley, mint, garlic, and oregano. Stir in the cucumber, tomato, red pepper, onion, and olives, coating ingredients thoroughly with dressing. Gently stir in the cheese. Season to taste with salt and pepper. Makes about 4 1/2 cups.

Tried & True

- Greek Shrimp Cocktail (page 133)
- Crostini with Feta & Greek Salsa (page 139)
- Cypress Swordfish with Greek Salsa (page 165)
- Coriander-Feta Chicken on Greek Salsa (page 171)
- Mediterranean Lamb Roast with Greek Salsa (page 219)
- Greek-Style Green Beans (page 239)

Something New

- Serve alongside or atop simple grilled fish, chicken breasts, or pork chops.
- Serve in a bowl surrounded with toasted pita chips.
- Serve atop burgers or stuff into pocket-bread sandwiches.
- Toss with cooked, chilled orzo, bulgur, or couscous for a refreshing side dish.

SPICED APPLE–PEAR CHUTNEY

2   FIRM BUT RIPE PEARS, PEELED, CORED AND
    CHOPPED
2   GRANNY SMITH APPLES, PEELED, CORED
    AND CHOPPED
1   LARGE SWEET OR RED ONION
1½ CUPS LIGHT BROWN SUGAR
1   CUP CHOPPED TOMATOES
1   CUP DRIED CRANBERRIES
½   CUP WHITE WINE VINEGAR
¼   CUP SHERRY VINEGAR
½   CUP DRY WHITE WINE, APPLE CIDER OR
    WATER

1   TABLESPOON MINCED FRESH GARLIC
1   TABLESPOON MINCED FRESH GINGER
1   TEASPOON SEA SALT
1   TEASPOON MUSTARD SEED
1   TEASPOON DRIED ORANGE PEEL
1   TEASPOON GROUND CORIANDER
½   TEASPOON ALLSPICE
½   TEASPOON CAYENNE PEPPER
½   TEASPOON FRESHLY GROUND PEPPER
⅛   TEASPOON GROUND CLOVES
⅛   TEASPOON GROUND NUTMEG

In a large, non-reactive saucepan combine all ingredients and bring to a boil over medium-high heat, stirring until the sugar dissolves. Reduce heat and simmer until apples, pears, and onion are soft and chutney is thick, about 1 hour. Cool to room temperature. Store airtight in the refrigerator for up to 2 months. Makes about 3 cups.

ROSEMARY-DRIED FRUIT CHUTNEY

$1^1/_2$ CUPS CHOPPED DRIED APRICOTS

$3/_4$ CUP DRIED CRANBERRIES

$3/_4$ CUP DRIED CHERRIES

$3/_4$ CUP CHOPPED DRIED FIGS

1 LARGE RED ONION, CHOPPED

$3/_4$ CUP WATER

$3/_4$ CUP CIDER VINEGAR

$2/_3$ CUP PACKED LIGHT BROWN SUGAR

2 TABLESPOONS MINCED FRESH ROSEMARY

1 TABLESPOON MINCED FRESH GARLIC

1 TEASPOON GRATED ZEST PLUS $1/_4$ CUP JUICE FROM 1 ORANGE

1 TEASPOON GRATED ZEST PLUS 1 TABLESPOON JUICE FROM 1 LEMON

1 TEASPOON SEA SALT

$1/_2$ TEASPOON CAYENNE PEPPER

$2/_3$ CUP SLIVERED ALMONDS, LIGHTLY TOASTED

In a large, non-reactive saucepan over medium-high heat combine all ingredients except almonds and bring to a boil, stirring until the sugar dissolves. Reduce heat and simmer until fruit and onion are soft and chutney is thick, about 40 minutes. Stir in the almonds. Cool to room temperature. Store airtight in the refrigerator for up to 2 months. Makes about 4 cups.

TRIED & TRUE

- Crostini with Brie & Chutney (page 139)
- Chutney Stuffed Brie en Croute (page 140)

SOMETHING NEW

- Serve chutneys alongside pork roasts or ham.
- Mix with cream cheese or mayonnaise and spread on turkey or ham sandwiches.
- Mix with chicken chunks, celery, scallions and mayo for chicken salad sandwiches.
- Mix with cream cheese or spoon over Brie and serve with crackers or baguette slices.
- Serve Spiced Apple-Pear Chutney with aged cheddar cheese and thin slices of pumpernickel bread.

COCONUT-CILANTRO CHUTNEY

$^1/_2$ CUP PLAIN YOGURT (NOT FAT FREE)
$^1/_2$ CUP SHREDDED, SWEETENED COCONUT
$^1/_4$ CUP CHOPPED FRESH CILANTRO

2 TABLESPOONS CHOPPED FRESH MINT
1 MINCED JALAPEÑO PEPPER (OPTIONAL)
SALT AND FRESHLY GROUND PEPPER

In a small bowl combine the yogurt, coconut, cilantro, mint, and jalapeño. Mix well. Season to taste with salt and pepper. Refrigerate for up to 3 hours. Makes about 1 cup.

PINEAPPLE-COCONUT RAITA

$^1/_2$ CUP PLAIN YOGURT (NOT FAT FREE)
$^1/_2$ CUP CHOPPED PINEAPPLE
$^1/_2$ CUP SHREDDED, SWEETENED COCONUT

$^1/_4$ CUP CHOPPED FRESH CILANTRO
2 TABLESPOONS CHOPPED FRESH MINT
SEA SALT AND FRESHLY GROUND PEPPER

In a small bowl combine the yogurt, pineapple, coconut, cilantro, and mint. Mix well. Season to taste with salt and pepper. Refrigerate for up to 2 hours. Makes about 1$^1/_2$ cups.

CUCUMBER-FENNEL TZATZIKI

1 CUP PLAIN YOGURT (NOT FAT FREE)
1 CUP SEEDED, DICED CUCUMBER
$^1/_2$ CUP MINCED FENNEL BULB
2 TABLESPOONS FINELY MINCED RED ONION
2 TABLESPOONS CHOPPED FENNEL FRONDS
2 TEASPOONS FRESH LEMON JUICE

1 TEASPOON GRATED LEMON ZEST
1 GARLIC CLOVE, MINCED
1 TO 2 TEASPOONS ALEPPO PEPPER (OPTIONAL)
SEA SALT AND FRESHLY GROUND PEPPER

In a small bowl combine the yogurt, cucumber, fennel bulb, onion, fennel fronds, lemon juice and zest, and garlic. Mix well. Add Aleppo pepper if desired and season to taste with salt and pepper. Refrigerate for up to 2 hours. Makes about 2 cups.

Fennel & Sun-Dried Tomato Tzatziki

1   RECIPE CUCUMBER-FENNEL TZATZIKI

$^1/_4$ CUP MINCED SUN-DRIED TOMATOES (OIL-
    PACKED, DRAINED)

In a small bowl combine all ingredients. Mix well. Refrigerate for up to 2 hours. Makes about $2^1/_4$ cups.

Tried & True
- Masala-Spiced Sea Bass with Pineapple-Coconut Raita (page 163)
- Swordfish Souvlaki with Fennel & Sun-Dried Tomato Tzatziki (page 166)
- Indian-Spiced Burgers with Coconut-Cilantro Chutney (page 212)
- Mediterranean Lamb Chops with Cucumber-Fennel Tzatziki (page 215)
- Lamb Tikka with Pineapple-Coconut Raita (page 216)
- Lamb Souvlaki with Fennel & Sun-Dried Tomato Tzatziki (page 216)

Something New
- Mix either tzatziki with cooked chicken or turkey chunks and serve in toasted pocket bread.
- Add $^1/_2$ cup crumbled feta cheese to either tzatziki and serve in a bowl surrounded by toasted pita chips.
- Mix raita or chutney with cooked chicken or turkey chunks and serve in pineapple boats.
- Any of the above would be a delicious accompaniment to grilled shrimp skewers.
- Serve any of the above alongside grilled lamb chops or kebobs.

Balsamic-Gorgonzola Onions

2	TABLESPOONS UNSALTED BUTTER, DIVIDED	1	TABLESPOON MINCED FRESH THYME
2	OUNCES PANCETTA, CHOPPED	2	TABLESPOONS BALSAMIC VINEGAR
1	LARGE SWEET ONION, HALVED LENGTHWISE AND THINLY SLICED	$^1/_3$	CUP CRUMBLED GORGONZOLA CHEESE (OR ANOTHER BLUE CHEESE)
2	TABLESPOONS MINCED FRESH ROSEMARY		FRESHLY GROUND PEPPER

In a medium skillet heat 1 tablespoon butter over medium heat. Add the pancetta, onions, rosemary, and thyme and cook for 20 minutes, stirring frequently, or until the onion is soft and lightly browned. Stir in the balsamic vinegar and continue to cook for 5 minutes. Remove from the heat and add the remaining 1 tablespoon butter and Gorgonzola, stirring until the cheese is melted. Season to taste with pepper. Refrigerate for up to 2 days. Warm slightly before serving. Makes about 1 cup.

Sweet & Savory Onion Jam

$^1/_4$	CUP UNSALTED BUTTER	1	TEASPOON SUGAR
1	TEASPOON GROUND CORIANDER	1	TABLESPOON BALSAMIC VINEGAR
4	GARLIC CLOVES, MINCED	1	TABLESPOON SHERRY VINEGAR
3	MEDIUM SWEET ONIONS OR RED ONIONS, HALVED LENGTHWISE AND THINLY SLICED	1	TABLESPOON CURRANT JELLY
			SEA SALT AND FRESHLY GROUND PEPPER

In a large skillet or Dutch oven melt the butter over medium heat. Add the coriander and stir for 30 seconds. Add the garlic and stir for 30 seconds. Stir in the onions, then sprinkle with sugar, cover, and cook for 5 minutes. Uncover the pan and continue to cook until the onions are lightly browned and very soft, about 30 minutes, stirring occasionally.

Add both vinegars and currant jelly and stir for 1 additional minute or until the jelly is fully melted. Season the onions to taste with salt and pepper. Refrigerate, airtight, for up to 2 weeks. Serve warm, cold, or at room temperature. Makes about $1^1/_2$ cups.

Tried & True

- Crostini with Gorgonzola & Onion Jam (page 139)
- Blue Cheese Stuffed Salmon Burgers with Wild Mushrooms & Onion Jam (page 153)
- Rosemary Grilled Rib-Eyes with Balsamic-Gorgonzola Onions (page 78)
- Scarborough Sirloin with Wild Mushrooms & Onion Jam (page 203)
- Beefy Blue Cheese & Bacon Burgers (page 213)
- Over-the-Top Fancy Schmancy Green Beans (page 239)

Something New

- Spread Sweet & Savory Onion Jam on roast beef sandwiches.
- Serve Sweet & Savory Onion Jam with assorted cheeses, sausages, and crackers.

ROASTED EGGPLANT–PEPPER RELISH

1	MEDIUM EGGPLANT, UNPEELED AND CUT INTO $1/2$-INCH CHUNKS (ABOUT 4 CUPS)	$1/4$	CUP EXTRA VIRGIN OLIVE OIL
1	LARGE RED BELL PEPPER, CUT INTO $1/2$-INCH CHUNKS		SEA SALT AND FRESHLY GROUND PEPPER
1	LARGE YELLOW BELL PEPPER, CUT INTO $1/2$-INCH CHUNKS	$1^{1}/_{2}$	TABLESPOONS PESTO (PAGE 104 OR STORE-BOUGHT)
1	LARGE SWEET ONION, CUT INTO $1/2$-INCH CHUNKS	1	TABLESPOON ROASTED GARLIC (PAGE 8 OR STORE-BOUGHT)

Preheat the oven to 425°.

Place the eggplant, bell peppers, and onions on a large, heavy baking sheet or roasting pan. Drizzle with olive oil and toss well to coat evenly. Sprinkle generously with salt and pepper. Roast in the center of the oven for 20 minutes. Remove the pan, stir, and return to the oven. Roast for an additional 20 minutes or until vegetables are soft and beginning to brown.

Remove mixture to a large bowl and mash lightly with a potato masher. Stir in the pesto and garlic. Makes about $1^{3}/_{4}$ cups.

Note: If you don't have any roasted garlic on hand, wrap a head in foil and toss it in the oven alongside the vegetables. Alternately, add $1^{1}/_{2}$ teaspoons minced fresh garlic to the vegetables during the second half of roasting.

ROASTED EGGPLANT–PEPPER TAPENADE

1	RECIPE ROASTED EGGPLANT-PEPPER RELISH	2	TABLESPOONS DRAINED, MINCED CAPERS
$1/2$	CUP PITTED, CHOPPED KALAMATA OR GAETA OLIVES	$1^{1}/_{2}$	TABLESPOONS GOOD BALSAMIC VINEGAR

In a medium bowl thoroughly mix all ingredients. Makes about 2 cups.

Roasted Eggplant-Pepper Caponata

1   RECIPE ROASTED EGGPLANT-PEPPER
    TAPENADE
1/2 CUP CHOPPED DRIED FIGS
1/2 CUP WATER
3   TABLESPOONS DRAINED, MINCED, OIL-
    PACKED SUN-DRIED TOMATOES

1   TEASPOON ANCHOVY PASTE (OPTIONAL)
1/4 TEASPOON RED PEPPER FLAKES
1/4 CUP CHOPPED ITALIAN PARSLEY
1/4 CUP TOASTED PINE NUTS

In a medium saucepan combine the tapenade, figs, water, tomatoes, anchovy paste, and pepper flakes. Bring to a simmer and simmer for 10 minutes, or until figs have softened slightly and mixture is thick. Remove from heat and stir in parsley and pine nuts. Makes about 3 cups.

Notes

Serve all of these recipes at room temperature. May be refrigerated, airtight, for up to 3 days.

Tried & True

- Crostini with Goat Cheese and Roasted Eggplant-Pepper Tapenade (page 138)
- Tapenade Filled Cheesecake (page 145)
- Sicilian Tuna Burgers with Caponata (page 161)
- Sicilian Swordfish with Caponata (page 165)
- Mozzarella Turkey Burgers with Eggplant-Pepper Topping (page 182)
- Caponata Pork Involtini (page 191)
- Sicilian Sirloin (page 203)
- Tuscan Inspired Green Beans (page 239)

Something New

- Use any of the relishes as a pizza topping, burger topping or sandwich spread.
- Toss Roasted Eggplant-Pepper Relish with pasta, tomato-basil flavored sausages and freshly grated Parmesan cheese.

Roasted Ratatouille Relish

$1^1/_2$ CUPS DICED, UNPEELED EGGPLANT

1   CUP DICED SWEET ONION OR RED ONION

1   CUP DICED ZUCCHINI

$^1/_2$ CUP DICED RED BELL PEPPER

$^1/_2$ CUP DICED YELLOW OR ORANGE BELL PEPPER

$^1/_4$ CUP EXTRA VIRGIN OLIVE OIL

2   TABLESPOONS CHOPPED FRESH OREGANO

2   TABLESPOONS BALSAMIC VINEGAR, PLUS MORE TO TASTE

SEA SALT AND FRESHLY GROUND PEPPER

$1^1/_2$ CUPS HALVED GRAPE TOMATOES (OR CHERRY TOMATOES)

1   TABLESPOON MINCED FLAT-LEAF PARSLEY

1   TABLESPOON MINCED FRESH BASIL

2   TEASPOONS MINCED FRESH GARLIC

Preheat the oven to 400°. Oil a large baking sheet (or use a nonstick baking sheet).

In a large bowl toss together the eggplant, onion, zucchini, bell peppers, olive oil, oregano, and 2 tablespoons vinegar. Season generously with salt and pepper. Spread mixture onto the prepared baking sheet and roast in the middle of the oven for 20 minutes.

Remove from the oven and stir in the tomatoes, parsley, basil, and garlic. Return to the oven and roast for an additional 20 minutes.

Place the relish in a bowl and season to taste with additional balsamic, salt, and pepper. If desired, lightly smash the vegetables with a fork or potato masher to achieve a more sauce-like texture. Makes about 3 cups.

Tried & True

- Provençal Fish Brochettes on Roasted Ratatouille Relish (page 167)
- Pesto Chicken on Roasted Ratatouille Relish (page 171)
- Provencal Pork Tenderloin with Roasted Ratatouille Relish (page 187)

Something New

- Use relish as a topping for toasted baguette slices.
- Toss relish with pasta dishes or scatter over pizza.
- Roasted Ratatouille Side Dish—Follow the directions for Roasted Rata-touille Relish, with the following changes: Double quantities of all ingredients; cut vegetables into larger chunks or slices; roast vegetables at 425° for slightly longer, until tender and lightly browned; if desired, top ratatouille with freshly grated Parmesan or crumbled feta cheese.

CHARRED PEPPER & ONION RELISH

1 MEDIUM SWEET ONION, THICKLY SLICED

1 LARGE RED BELL PEPPER, QUARTERED, SEEDS AND VEINS REMOVED

1 LARGE YELLOW BELL PEPPER, QUARTERED, SEEDS AND VEINS REMOVED

2 TO 3 TABLESPOONS OLIVE OIL
SEA SALT AND FRESHLY GROUND PEPPER

2 TEASPOONS BALSAMIC VINEGAR

1 TEASPOON ROASTED GARLIC (PAGE 8 OR STORE-BOUGHT) OR $1/2$ TEASPOON MINCED FRESH GARLIC

1 TEASPOON SUGAR

1 TEASPOON GROUND CORIANDER

$1/4$ TEASPOON GROUND CAYENNE, OR TO TASTE

Preheat the grill to medium-high heat.

Brush the onion slices and peppers with oil, season lightly with salt and pepper, and place them directly on the grill rack or on a perforated grill pan. (If not using a grill pan, thread the onion slices onto long metal skewers to keep them together.) Grill the vegetables until softened and slightly charred, about 15 minutes, turning and moving around grill as needed. Remove from the grill, let cool slightly, and chop roughly. Combine chopped onion and peppers with remaining relish ingredients and season to taste with additional salt and pepper.

NOTES

This relish can also be prepared using the broiler. Broil the onion and peppers about 6 inches from the flame and watch them carefully.

TRIED & TRUE

- Crostini with Queso Fresco and Charred Pepper & Onion Relish (page 139)
- Goat Cheese Stuffed Turkey Burgers with Charred Pepper & Onion Relish (page 182)

SOMETHING NEW

- Toss with bowtie pasta, grilled sausage, or chicken breast slices and feta cheese for a delicious and hearty dinner entrée.
- Serve over thinly sliced grilled flank steak or sirloin.
- Serve as a topping for hamburgers, cheeseburgers, hot dogs, or bratwurst.

WILD MUSHROOM SAUTÉ

1 TABLESPOON OLIVE OIL

4 OUNCES PANCETTA, CHOPPED

1/4 CUP MINCED SHALLOTS

1 TABLESPOON MINCED FRESH GARLIC

1 POUND CREMINI (BABY PORTABELLA) MUSHROOMS, HALVED AND THINLY SLICED

1/2 POUND SHIITAKE MUSHROOM CAPS, HALVED IF LARGE AND THINLY SLICED

2 TABLESPOONS MINCED FRESH THYME

1/2 CUP MEDIUM DRY SHERRY OR MADEIRA

1/2 CUP HEAVY CREAM OR HALF & HALF

1 TABLESPOON MINCED FRESH CHIVES (OPTIONAL)

1 TEASPOON GRATED LEMON ZEST

SEA SALT AND FRESHLY GROUND PEPPER

In a large skillet or Dutch oven heat the olive oil over medium heat. Add the pancetta and shallots and sauté for 5 minutes. Add the garlic and sauté for 1 minute. Stir in the mushrooms and thyme, cover the pan, and cook for 3 minutes. Remove the cover, increase the heat to medium high, and sauté for an additional 12 minutes or until the mushrooms are beginning to brown and all liquid has evaporated, stirring frequently.

Stir in the sherry and simmer for 5 minutes or until completely evaporated. Stir in the cream and simmer for 2 minutes. Remove from the heat and stir in the chives and lemon zest. Season to taste with salt and pepper. Refrigerate for up to 2 days. Serve warm. Makes about 4 cups.

Notes

If desired, replace half of the cremini mushrooms with another mushroom, such as chanterelles, morels, or oyster mushrooms.

Tried & True

- Crostini with Goat Cheese & Wild Mushrooms (page 139)
- Wild Mushroom Stuffed Brie en Croute (page 141)
- Blue Cheese Stuffed Salmon Burgers with Onion Jam & Wild Mushrooms (page 153)
- Scarborough Sirloin with Wild Mushrooms & Onion Jam (page 203)
- Wild Mushroom Smashed Potatoes (page 231)

Something New

- Toss with cooked pasta, such as penne, for an earthy accompaniment to roast pork or chicken.
- Toss with cooked bowtie pasta, chicken & apple sausages, and freshly grated Parmesan cheese for a lusty dinner entrée.
- Serve alongside grilled steaks, lamb chops, salmon steaks, or pork tenderloin.

Gremolata

$1/4$ CUP MINCED FRESH ITALIAN PARSLEY

2 TEASPOONS GRATED LEMON ZEST

1 TEASPOON MINCED FRESH GARLIC

SEA SALT

In a small bowl toss together the parsley, lemon zest, and garlic. Season lightly with sea salt.

Sesame-Scallion Gremolata

$1/2$ CUP MINCED SCALLIONS, WHITE AND LIGHT
GREEN PARTS ONLY

$1^1/2$ TABLESPOONS TOASTED SESAME SEEDS

1 TEASPOON MINCED FRESH GARLIC

1 TEASPOON GRATED FRESH LIME ZEST

SEA SALT

In a small bowl toss together the scallions, sesame seeds, garlic, and lime zest. Season lightly with sea salt.

Orange-Chive Gremolata

2 TABLESPOONS MINCED FRESH CHIVES

2 TABLESPOONS MINCED ITALIAN PARSLEY

2 TEASPOONS GRATED FRESH ORANGE ZEST

1 TEASPOON MINCED FRESH GARLIC

SEA SALT

In a small bowl toss together the chives, parsley, orange zest, and garlic. Season lightly with sea salt.

Golden Gremolata

2   TABLESPOONS EXTRA VIRGIN OLIVE OIL
¼   CUP MINCED SHALLOTS
2   TEASPOONS MINCED FRESH GARLIC
1   CUP FRESH BREADCRUMBS

¼   CUP MINCED FRESH ITALIAN PARSLEY
2   TEASPOONS FRESHLY GRATED LEMON ZEST
    SEA SALT

In a medium sauté pan heat the olive oil over medium-high heat. Add the shallots and sauté for 2 minutes. Add the garlic and sauté for 1 minute. Add the breadcrumbs and sauté for 3 minutes or until golden and crisp. Remove from the heat and stir in the parsley and lemon zest. Season lightly with sea salt.

Tried & True

Miso Grilled Salmon with Sesame-Scallion Gremolata (page 154)
Orange-Bourbon Grilled Salmon (page 155)
Citrus & Garlic Green Beans (page 239)
Sesame-Scallion Green Beans (page 239)

Something New

- Sprinkle Gremolata over roasted leg of lamb.
- Toss Sesame-Scallion Gremolata with cooked rice or noodles for an Asian-inspired side dish.
- Scatter Sesame-Scallion Gremolata over teriyaki-marinated shrimp skewers for a great appetizer.
- Sprinkle Golden Gremolata over cooked vegetables such as broccoli, cauliflower, beans, or asparagus.
- Toss Golden Gremolata over sautéed shrimp or scallops.
- Sprinkle Golden Gremolata over any pasta dish.

SAUCES, VINAIGRETTES, AND GLAZES

The sauces here encompass a wide variety of flavors, using ingredients such as sweet dried fruits, savory mushrooms and tomatoes, tangy citrus and aromatic herbs. You'll find many uses for them, in addition to the recipes in the book.

All of the recipes in this section can be prepared up to one day in advance and stored, covered, in the refrigerator.

CHERRY-PORT SAUCE

Be sure to use a good quality tawny port here, to ensure a great tasting sauce. Serve the rest of the bottle with chocolate cake for dessert—Yum!

1	TABLESPOON OLIVE OIL
1	TABLESPOON UNSALTED BUTTER
$1/4$	CUP MINCED SHALLOTS
4	GARLIC CLOVES, MINCED
2	TEASPOONS MINCED FRESH THYME LEAVES
$1/4$	CUP BALSAMIC VINEGAR
$2/3$	CUP TAWNY PORT

$1^1/4$	CUPS LOW-SODIUM CHICKEN BROTH OR HOMEMADE STOCK
$1/2$	CUP DRIED TART CHERRIES
1	BAY LEAF
1	TEASPOON CORNSTARCH MIXED WITH 1 TEASPOON WATER
2	TEASPOONS DIJON MUSTARD

In a medium saucepan melt the butter and oil over medium heat. Add the shallots, garlic, and thyme and sauté for 3 minutes. Add the balsamic vinegar and cook for 1 minute. Add the port, broth, cherries, and bay leaf, and bring to a boil; boil for 8 minutes. Whisk in the cornstarch mixture and cook, stirring constantly, for an additional 2 minutes. Remove from the heat and whisk in the mustard. Serves 4 to 6.

CHERRY-PORT SAUCE WITH PANCETTA & WILD MUSHROOMS

1 TABLESPOON OLIVE OIL	1/4 CUP BALSAMIC VINEGAR
3 OUNCES CHOPPED PANCETTA	2/3 CUP TAWNY PORT
4 OUNCES SHIITAKE MUSHROOM CAPS, THINLY SLICED	1 1/4 CUPS LOW-SODIUM CHICKEN BROTH OR HOMEMADE STOCK
4 OUNCES CREMINI MUSHROOMS, THINLY SLICED	1/2 CUP DRIED TART CHERRIES
1/2 CUP THINLY SLICED SHALLOTS	1 BAY LEAF
4 GARLIC CLOVES, MINCED	1 TEASPOON CORNSTARCH MIXED WITH 1 TEASPOON WATER
1 TABLESPOON MINCED FRESH THYME LEAVES	1 TEASPOON DIJON MUSTARD

In a large, heavy saucepan heat the oil over medium heat. Add the pancetta and sauté until it begins to brown, about 4 minutes. Remove with a slotted spoon and set aside. Discard all but 1 tablespoon of oil. Add the mushrooms, shallots, garlic, and thyme leaves and sauté until all of the liquid released by the mushrooms has evaporated and the mushrooms are beginning to brown, about 8 minutes. Add the balsamic vinegar, scrape up the browned bits, and cook for 1 minute. Add the port, broth, cherries, and bay leaf; bring to a boil. Boil for 8 minutes. Whisk in the cornstarch mixture and cook, stirring, for an additional 2 minutes. Remove from the heat and whisk in the mustard. Serves 4 to 6.

TRIED & TRUE

- Ancho-Spiced Salmon with Cherry-Port Sauce (page 151)
- Cherry Infused Game Hens with Smashed Potatoes (page 181)
- Rosemary-Thyme Pork Tenderloin with Cherry-Port Sauce (page 189)
- Ancho-Cinnamon Flank Steak with Cherry-Port Sauce (page 205)

SOMETHING NEW

- Serve either of the sauces over a leg of lamb or prime rib roast.
- Cherry-Port Sauce with Pancetta & Wild Mushrooms is a sure-fire way to liven up a simple baked ham.

CRANBERRY-PORT SAUCE

Marinate pork, beef or lamb in Red Wine-Orange Marinade (page 26) for 2 to 4 hours before starting on this mouthwatering sauce.

1   CUP RED WINE-ORANGE MARINADE (RESERVED FROM MARINATING MEAT), STRAINED, SOLIDS DISCARDED (PAGE 26)

1   CUP LOW SODIUM CHICKEN BROTH OR HOMEMADE STOCK

$1/2$ CUP RUBY PORT

$1/2$ CUP DRIED CRANBERRIES

$1^1/2$ TEASPOONS CORNSTARCH

2   TABLESPOONS UNSALTED BUTTER

1   TABLESPOON BALSAMIC VINEGAR
    SEA SALT AND FRESHLY GROUND PEPPER

In a medium saucepan bring the marinade and broth to a boil over medium-high heat; boil gently until reduced by half, about 12 minutes. Stir in the port and cranberries and boil 5 minutes. Combine the cornstarch with 2 teaspoons water and whisk into the sauce. Cook for 2 more minutes, whisking constantly. Remove the sauce from heat and stir in the butter and balsamic. Season to taste with salt and pepper. Makes about 2 cups.

CRANBERRY–PORT SAUCE II

If you'd like to make the sauce without using the marinade, here's your option.

2	TABLESPOONS OLIVE OIL	$1/2$	CUP RUBY PORT
$1/4$	CUP MINCED SHALLOTS	$1/2$	CUP DRIED CRANBERRIES
1	TABLESPOON MINCED FRESH GARLIC	$1^1/2$	TEASPOONS CORNSTARCH
1	TABLESPOON FRESH THYME LEAVES	2	TABLESPOONS UNSALTED BUTTER
1	BAY LEAF	1	TABLESPOON BALSAMIC VINEGAR
$1/2$	TEASPOON MUSTARD SEED		SEA SALT AND FRESHLY GROUND PEPPER
1	CUP DRY RED WINE		
$1^1/4$	CUPS LOW SODIUM CHICKEN BROTH OR HOMEMADE STOCK		

In a medium saucepan heat the olive oil over medium heat. Add the shallots and garlic and sauté for 4 minutes. Add the thyme, bay leaf, and mustard seed and cook for 1 minute. Add the wine and broth; bring to a boil over medium-high heat. Boil gently until reduced by half, about 15 minutes. Strain the mixture, pressing hard on the solids. Discard the solids and return the liquid to pan. Stir in the port and cranberries; return to a gentle boil for 5 minutes. Combine the cornstarch with 2 teaspoons water and whisk into the sauce. Cook for 2 more minutes, whisking constantly. Remove the sauce from the heat and stir in the butter and balsamic. Season to taste with salt and pepper. Makes about 2 cups.

TRIED & TRUE

- Orange Infused Pork Tenderloin with Cranberry-Port Sauce (page 187)
- Orange Infused Lamb Chops with Cranberry-Port Sauce (page 215)

SOMETHING NEW

- Try marinating a venison roast in Red Wine-Orange Marinade and serving with Cranberry-Port Sauce.
- Serve Cranberry Port Sauce II with simple roast chicken, game hens, or turkey.

RED WINE-PORT SAUCE

Marinate beef or lamb in Scarborough Fair Marinade (page 27) for 4 to 12 hours before making this rich and luxurious sauce.

1   CUP STRAINED SCARBOROUGH FAIR
    MARINADE (PAGE 27), RESERVED FROM
    MARINATING MEAT
1   CUP RUBY PORT
1   CUP LOW SODIUM BEEF BROTH OR
    HOMEMADE STOCK

1   CUP LOW SODIUM CHICKEN BROTH OR
    HOMEMADE STOCK
2   TABLESPOONS UNSALTED BUTTER, SOFTENED
1½ TABLESPOONS FLOUR
1   TABLESPOON CURRANT JELLY

In a medium saucepan bring the marinade and port to a boil over medium-high heat and boil until reduced to 1 cup, about 13 to 15 minutes, skimming any foam. Add the beef broth and chicken broth; boil over medium-high heat until reduced to 1½ cups, about 17 to 20 minutes. Mash together the butter and flour and whisk into the sauce; reduce the heat to medium and cook for 2 minutes. Remove from the heat and whisk in the currant jelly. Makes about 1½ cups.

Red Wine-Port Sauce II

If you'd like to make the sauce without using the marinade, this option is equally delicious.

2   TABLESPOONS OLIVE OIL
1/4 CUP MINCED SHALLOTS
1   TABLESPOON CHOPPED FRESH GARLIC
2   TABLESPOONS FRESH THYME LEAVES
1   TABLESPOON CHOPPED FRESH SAGE
1   CUP DRY RED WINE
1   CUP RUBY PORT

1   CUP LOW SODIUM BEEF BROTH OR HOMEMADE STOCK
1   CUP LOW SODIUM CHICKEN BROTH OR HOMEMADE STOCK
2   TABLESPOONS UNSALTED BUTTER, SOFTENED
1 1/2 TABLESPOONS FLOUR
1   TABLESPOON CURRANT JELLY

In a medium saucepan heat the olive oil over medium heat. Add the shallots and garlic and sauté for 4 minutes. Add the thyme and sage and sauté for 1 minute. Add the wine and port, bring to a boil, and boil over medium-high heat until reduced to 1 1/4 cups, about 13 to 15 minutes. Add the beef broth and chicken broth; boil over medium-high heat until reduced to 1 3/4 cups, about 17 to 20 minutes. Strain mixture, discarding solids; return to pan and place over medium heat. Mash together butter and flour and whisk into sauce. Cook for 2 minutes. Remove from heat and whisk in currant jelly. Makes about 1 1/2 cups.

Tried & True

Roasted Leg of Lamb with Red Wine-Port Sauce (page 218)

Something New

Try with prime rib roast, beef tenderloin roast, bacon-wrapped filet mignon or grilled steaks.

RED WINE-PEPPER SAUCE

3   TABLESPOONS UNSALTED BUTTER, DIVIDED
¾ CUP MINCED SHALLOTS
1   CUP CHOPPED ROASTED RED BELL PEPPERS
     (PAGE 9 OR STORE-BOUGHT)
1   CUP DRY RED WINE

1   CUP LOW SODIUM CHICKEN BROTH OR
     HOMEMADE STOCK
1   TABLESPOON BALSAMIC VINEGAR
     SEA SALT AND FRESHLY GROUND PEPPER

In a medium skillet heat 2 tablespoons butter over medium heat. Add the shallots and sauté 5 minutes. Add the bell peppers and sauté 3 minutes. Add the wine, bring to a boil, and boil for 5 minutes or until almost evaporated. Add the broth, return to a boil for 5 minutes. Carefully transfer the mixture to a blender or food processor and purée. Return the sauce to the pan and whisk in the remaining 1 tablespoon butter and balsamic. Season to taste with salt and pepper. Makes about 2 cups.

Roasted Garlic, Red Wine & Pepper Sauce

1   RECIPE RED WINE-PEPPER SAUCE
2   TABLESPOONS ROASTED GARLIC (PAGE 8 OR
    STORE-BOUGHT)

Follow the directions for Red Wine-Pepper Sauce, adding the roasted garlic to the blender or processor along with the sauce. Purée the mixture and continue with the recipe as directed. Makes about 2 cups.

Tried & True

- Herb Crusted Pork Tenderloin with Roasted Garlic, Red Wine & Pepper Sauce (page 189)
- Herbed Flank Steak Roulade with Red Pepper–Wine Sauce (page 208)

Something New

- Try Red Wine-Pepper Sauce on grilled steaks rubbed with garlic & rosemary before grilling.
- Serve either sauce with lamb chops or veal chops.
- Brush Roasted Garlic, Red Wine & Pepper Sauce over meatloaf during the last 30 minutes of baking.

Red Wine Marinara

Each September I make tons of this sauce with fresh tomatoes and herbs from our garden and freeze it to enjoy all winter long. Keep some gourmet sausages in the freezer and a variety of pasta shapes in the pantry, and you'll have the makings for delicious dinners in a snap.

2   TABLESPOONS OLIVE OIL

1¹/₂ CUPS CHOPPED ONION

¹/₂ CUP CHOPPED GREEN OR YELLOW BELL PEPPER

¹/₂ CUP PEELED, CHOPPED CARROT

4   OUNCES SLICED CREMINI MUSHROOMS

5   LARGE GARLIC CLOVES, MINCED

1   CUP DRY RED WINE

4   CUPS PEELED, SEEDED, CHOPPED TOMATOES*

¹/₂ CUP LOW SODIUM CHICKEN BROTH OR HOMEMADE STOCK

1   6-OUNCE CAN ROASTED GARLIC FLAVORED TOMATO PASTE

¹/₄ CUP CHOPPED FRESH BASIL, DIVIDED

2   TABLESPOONS CHOPPED FRESH OREGANO OR 2 TEASPOONS DRIED

1   TABLESPOON CHOPPED FRESH ROSEMARY OR 1 TEASPOON DRIED

1   TABLESPOON BALSAMIC VINEGAR

¹/₂ TABLESPOON SUGAR

¹/₂ TEASPOON SEA SALT OR KOSHER SALT

¹/₂ TEASPOON CRUSHED RED PEPPER

¹/₄ TEASPOON CRACKED PEPPER

In a large saucepan heat the oil over medium heat. Add the onion, bell pepper, and carrot and sauté for 5 minutes. Add the mushrooms and garlic and sauté for 10 minutes. Add the wine and scrape up any browned bits. Add the tomatoes and chicken broth and bring to a boil. Stir in the tomato paste, 2 tablespoons basil, oregano, rosemary, vinegar, sugar, salt, and both peppers. Simmer, partially covered, for 20 minutes. Stir in the remaining basil. Correct the seasoning as desired. Makes about 6 cups. *Note:* Fresh tomatoes may be substituted with 2 14-ounce cans diced tomatoes, undrained.

Tried & True

- Mussels Marinara (page 135)
- Bruschetta Chicken Pasta (page 173)

Something New

- Toss with penne and serve alongside any of the stuffed pork tenderloin recipes on pages 190–91.
- Use to make lasagna, chicken cacciatore, spaghetti & meatballs, or any dish in which you might be tempted to use a jar of supermarket pasta sauce.
- Add 1 tablespoon ground fennel seed or $1/4$ cup chopped fresh tarragon and use as a sauce for homemade pizza.

Orange Romesco Sauce

1 CUP FRESH ORANGE JUICE	$^1/_4$ CUP WALNUT OIL
1 BAY LEAF (MEDITERRANEAN)	1 TABLESPOON SHERRY VINEGAR
1 CUP CHOPPED ROASTED RED BELL PEPPERS (PAGE 9 OR STORE-BOUGHT)	$^1/_2$ TEASPOON SPANISH SMOKED PAPRIKA (PIMENTÓN)
2 TABLESPOONS MINCED SHALLOT	1 TABLESPOON UNSALTED BUTTER
2 TABLESPOONS TOMATO PASTE	SEA SALT AND FRESHLY GROUND PEPPER

Place the orange juice and bay leaf in a medium saucepan and bring to a boil over medium-high heat. Boil gently until reduced to $^1/_2$ cup, about 10 minutes. Add the red peppers, shallot, and tomato paste, whisking to incorporate the tomato paste, and boil for 5 more minutes.

Carefully transfer the mixture to a processor or blender. Add the walnut oil, sherry vinegar, and paprika, and purée. Return the mixture to the saucepan, whisk in 1 tablespoon butter, and season to taste with salt and pepper. Makes about 2 cups.

Curried Orange-Apricot Sauce

2 TABLESPOONS OLIVE OIL	$^1/_4$ CUP APRICOT PRESERVES, LARGE APRICOT PIECES CHOPPED
$^1/_4$ CUP MINCED SHALLOTS	$^1/_8$ TEASPOON CAYENNE PEPPER
1 TEASPOON SWEET CURRY POWDER	$1^1/_2$ TEASPOON CORNSTARCH
1 CUP FRESH ORANGE JUICE	
1 CUP PLUS 1 TABLESPOON LOW SODIUM CHICKEN BROTH OR HOMEMADE STOCK, DIVIDED	

In a medium saucepan heat the olive oil over medium heat. Add the shallots and sauté for 3 minutes. Stir in the curry powder and cook for 1 minute. Add the orange juice and 1 cup of the chicken broth; increase the heat and boil until reduced by half, about 10 minutes. Reduce heat to medium and whisk in the apricot preserves and cayenne. In a small bowl whisk together the cornstarch and remaining 1 tablespoon chicken broth, and whisk into the sauce. Cook for 2 minutes or until thick and bubbly. Makes about $1^1/_2$ cups.

Tried & True

- Spice Dusted Salmon with Curried Orange-Apricot Sauce (page 150)
- Seed Crusted Salmon with Orange Romesco Sauce (page 151)
- Seed Crusted Pork Tenderloin with Orange Romesco Sauce (page 188)
- Moroccan Spiced Lamb Kabobs with Curried Orange-Apricot Sauce (page 217)

Something New

- Serve Orange Romesco Sauce as a dipping sauce for shrimp sautéed with garlic.
- Serve Curried Orange-Apricot Sauce as a dipping sauce for grilled shrimp and pineapple skewers.
- Serve either sauce over pan-seared chicken or duck breasts coated with Mediterranean Seed Crust (page 38) or Toasted Mustard Seed Crust (page 38).
- Serve either sauce with grilled or pan seared pork chops, scallops, swordfish, or tuna.
- For a new twist on the Curried Orange-Apricot Sauce, try replacing the orange juice with pineapple juice or replacing the apricot preserves with pineapple preserves.

BASIL-MINT PESTO

I make a double batch of this delicious pesto at the end of every summer, when the garden is overflowing with basil and mint, and freeze it in ¹/₄–¹/₂ cup plastic containers. That way, I can enjoy the garden-fresh taste of summer all winter long!

6	CUPS PACKED FRESH BASIL LEAVES	2	TABLESPOONS FRESH LEMON JUICE
2	CUPS PACKED FRESH MINT LEAVES	1¹/₂	CUPS FRESHLY GRATED PARMIGIANO-REGGIANO
²/₃	CUP EXTRA VIRGIN OLIVE OIL		
¹/₂	CUP LIGHTLY TOASTED PINENUTS		SEA SALT AND FRESHLY GROUND PEPPER
¹/₄	CUP MINCED FRESH GARLIC		

Plunge the basil and mint leaves into a large pot of boiling water for 10 seconds. Drain and plunge into a large bowl of ice water to stop the cooking and set the color. Drain and squeeze dry.

Put the basil, mint, olive oil, pinenuts, garlic, and lemon juice in a food processor and purée. Add the cheese and pulse to combine. Season to taste with salt and pepper. Makes about 2 cups.

CHIMICHURRI SAUCE

2	CUPS ITALIAN PARSLEY LEAVES, PACKED	1	TABLESPOON FRESH LIME JUICE
6	CLOVES GARLIC, CHOPPED	2	TEASPOONS DRIED OREGANO
4	SCALLIONS, CHOPPED	¹/₂	TO 1 TEASPOON RED PEPPER FLAKES
¹/₂	CUP EXTRA VIRGIN OLIVE OIL		SEA SALT AND FRESHLY GROUND PEPPER
¹/₄	CUP RED WINE VINEGAR		

In a food processor combine the parsley, garlic, scallions, olive oil, vinegar, lime juice, oregano, and red pepper flakes and process until fairly smooth. Season to taste with salt and pepper. Makes about 1¹/₂ cups.

NOTES

Pesto will keep, airtight, in the refrigerator for 2 weeks or in the freezer for 8 months.

TRIED & TRUE

- Roasted Eggplant-Pepper Relish/Tapenade/Caponata (pages 80–81)
- Chimichurri Chicken Skewers (page 137)
- Pesto Chicken on Ratatouille Relish (page 171)
- Argentine Flank Steak with Chimichurri Sauce (page 204)
- Argentina-Style Flank Steak . . . Matambre (page 209)
- Chile-Fired Burgers with Chimichurri (page 213)
- Pesto Stuffed Baked Potatoes (page 228)

SOMETHING NEW

- Combine pesto with goat cheese or cream cheese and minced sun-dried tomatoes. Serve with crackers or baguette slices.
- Whisk pesto with a splash of balsamic vinegar and toss with oven-roasted potatoes.
- Toss pesto with sautéed zucchini, yellow squash, sliced onion, and sliced bell peppers for a delicious summery side dish.

Sherried Mushroom & Caramelized Onion Sauce

1 TABLESPOON UNSALTED BUTTER

1 TABLESPOON OLIVE OIL

1 LARGE SWEET ONION, HALVED AND THINLY SLICED

4 OUNCES CREMINI MUSHROOMS, SLICED

4 OUNCES SHIITAKE MUSHROOM CAPS, SLICED

1 TABLESPOON MINCED FRESH THYME LEAVES

$3/4$ CUP MEDIUM DRY (AMONTILLADO OR MANZANILLA) SHERRY

$1^{1}/_{4}$ CUPS LOW SODIUM CHICKEN BROTH

$1^{1}/_{4}$ CUPS LOW SODIUM BEEF BROTH

$1/2$ TABLESPOON ROASTED GARLIC (PAGE 8 OR STORE-BOUGHT)

1 TABLESPOON FLOUR

1 TABLESPOON UNSALTED BUTTER, SOFTENED

$1/4$ CUP CHOPPED ITALIAN PARSLEY FRESHLY GROUND PEPPER

In a large, wide saucepan or skillet melt the butter in oil over medium heat. Add the onions; cover and cook for 5 minutes. Add the mushrooms and thyme; cover and cook for 3 minutes. Uncover; raise the heat to medium high and cook for 15 minutes or until onions are very soft and golden brown.

Add the sherry and cook until almost evaporated, 2 to 3 minutes. Add the chicken and beef broth, bring to a boil, and boil for 10 minutes or until reduced by about half. Mash together the garlic, flour, and softened butter and whisk into the sauce. Cook for 2 minutes, stirring frequently. Remove sauce from the heat and stir in the parsley. Season to taste with pepper. Makes about 3 cups.

TRIED & TRUE

Herb Crusted Pork Tenderloin with Mushroom & Onion Sauce (page 189)

SOMETHING NEW

- Spoon sauce over baked or mashed potatoes.
- Try with beef tenderloin, veal, roast chicken, turkey, or game hens.
- Serve over pan-seared salmon on a bed of egg noodles.

Sesame-Soy Dipping Sauce

²/₃ CUP SOY SAUCE

6 TABLESPOONS SAKE OR DRY SHERRY

¹/₄ CUP SUGAR

8 SCALLIONS, MINCED, WHITE AND MOST OF
GREEN PARTS

2 TABLESPOONS ASIAN SESAME OIL

2 TABLESPOONS TOASTED SESAME SEEDS

2 TEASPOONS RICE VINEGAR

Whisk together first 3 ingredients, dissolving sugar. Whisk in remaining ingredients. Makes about 2¹/₄ cups. Sauce may be refrigerated, covered, for up to 2 days.

Pineapple-Sesame Dipping Sauce

1 RECIPE SESAME-SOY DIPPING SAUCE

1 CUP CHOPPED FRESH PINEAPPLE

Stir pineapple into dipping sauce. Makes about 3¹/₄ cups.

Spicy Sesame-Soy Dipping Sauce

1 RECIPE SESAME-SOY DIPPING SAUCE

2 TO 3 TABLESPOONS ASIAN CHILE SAUCE

Whisk chile sauce into dipping sauce. Makes about 2¹/₄ cups.

Tried & True

- Korean-Style Lettuce Wraps with Sesame-Soy Dipping Sauce (page 206)
- Teriyaki Lettuce Wraps (page 207)

Something New

- Serve any of the dipping sauces with spring rolls or egg rolls.
- Serve any of the sauces with grilled or pan-seared salmon, tuna, or shrimp.
- Drizzle Sesame-Soy Dipping Sauce over grilled or roasted asparagus or eggplant.

Spicy Peanut Dipping Sauce

1¹/₂ TABLESPOONS PEANUT OIL OR CANOLA OIL

¹/₂ CUP MINCED ONION

1 TABLESPOON MINCED FRESH GINGER

1 TABLESPOON MINCED FRESH GARLIC

³/₄ CUP COCONUT MILK

¹/₄ CUP CREAMY PEANUT BUTTER

2 TABLESPOONS LIGHT BROWN SUGAR

2 TABLESPOONS SOY SAUCE

2 TABLESPOONS FRESH JUICE PLUS GRATED ZEST FROM 1 LIME

1 TABLESPOON OYSTER SAUCE

1 TABLESPOON RICE VINEGAR

1 TABLESPOON ASIAN CHILE SAUCE, OR MORE TO TASTE

In a small saucepan heat the oil over medium heat. Add the onion, ginger, and garlic and sauté until softened, about 7 minutes. Add the coconut milk and bring to a simmer. Remove from the heat and add the peanut butter and brown sugar, whisking to dissolve the sugar. Whisk in the remaining ingredients. Serve at room temperature. Makes about 2 cups.

Tried & True

- Thai Coconut Chicken Sate with Spicy Peanut Dipping Sauce (page 137)
- Thai Lemongrass Lettuce Wraps with Spicy Peanut Dipping Sauce (page 207)

Something New

- Makes a great dipping sauce for take-out egg rolls and spring rolls.
- Wrap shrimp or scallops in bacon; skewer and grill. Drizzle with peanut sauce.
- Toss sauce with soba noodles and minced scallions. Chill and serve as a side dish with grilled pork, chicken, or salmon that has been marinated in any of the Thai marinades on pages 14–15.

Ponzu Dipping Sauce

$^1/_4$ CUP SOY SAUCE

$^1/_4$ CUP MIRIN

2 TABLESPOONS FROZEN ORANGE JUICE
CONCENTRATE, THAWED

2 TABLESPOONS FRESH LEMON JUICE

1 TEASPOON MINCED FRESH GINGER

4 MINCED SCALLIONS, WHITE AND LIGHT
GREEN PARTS ONLY, DIVIDED

$^1/_2$ TEASPOON CRUSHED RED PEPPER

In a small saucepan combine the soy sauce, mirin, orange juice concentrate, lemon juice, ginger, and half of the scallions. Bring to a boil over medium heat and boil for 3 minutes. Remove from the heat and stir in the remaining scallions and red pepper. Makes about $^3/_4$ cup.

Wasabi Ponzu

Whisk 1–1$^1/_2$ tablespoons wasabi paste in to Ponzu Dipping Sauce after boiling. Omit crushed red pepper if desired. Makes about $^3/_4$ cup.

Tried & True

- Sesame Seared Tuna with Wasabi Mayo & Ponzu Dipping Sauce (page 159)
- Teriyaki Lettuce Wraps with Wasabi Ponzu (page 207)

Something New

- Serve Wasabi Ponzu as a dipping sauce with takeout or homemade sushi.
- Mix with a little cornstarch with cooled Ponzu Dipping Sauce and add to stir-fried vegetables toward the end of cooking.

Sautéed Mushroom Vinaigrette

2   TABLESPOONS OLIVE OIL
4   OUNCES SHIITAKE MUSHROOM CAPS, THINLY SLICED
4   OUNCES CREMINI MUSHROOMS, THINLY SLICED
1/2 CUP THINLY SLICED SHALLOTS
1 1/2 TABLESPOONS MINCED FRESH GARLIC
1/2 CUP MEDIUM DRY (AMONTILLADO) SHERRY (OR DRY SHERRY)
1/2 CUP CHICKEN BROTH

1/4 CUP RED WINE VINEGAR
1   TABLESPOON MINCED FRESH THYME
2   TABLESPOONS GRAINY DIJON MUSTARD
1   TABLESPOON HONEY
1/3 CUP EXTRA VIRGIN OLIVE OIL
1/4 CUP WALNUT OIL
2   TABLESPOONS MINCED FRESH ITALIAN PARSLEY
1   TEASPOON GRATED FRESH LEMON ZEST
    SEA SALT AND FRESHLY GROUND PEPPER

In a large skillet heat the olive oil over medium-high heat. Add the mushrooms and sauté until the liquid has evaporated, about 7 minutes. Add the shallots and garlic and sauté for 5 minutes. Add the sherry, broth, vinegar, and thyme, and simmer until the liquid has reduced by half, about 6 minutes. Remove from heat. Gradually whisk in the mustard and honey, then both oils. Stir in the parsley and lemon zest. Season to taste with salt and pepper. Makes about 2 cups.

TWO-TOMATO VINAIGRETTE

¼ CUP FRUITY EXTRA VIRGIN OLIVE OIL

¼ CUP CHOPPED SHALLOTS

1 TABLESPOON MINCED FRESH GARLIC

1½ CUPS HALVED CHERRY TOMATOES

1½ CUPS HALVED YELLOW PEAR TOMATOES

2 TABLESPOONS WHITE BALSAMIC VINEGAR

1 TABLESPOON SUGAR

SEA SALT AND FRESHLY GROUND PEPPER

2 TABLESPOONS CHOPPED FRESH BASIL

In a medium sauté pan heat the olive oil over medium heat. Add the shallots and garlic and sauté for 3 minutes. Add the tomatoes and sauté for 3 minutes. Add the vinegar and sugar and simmer for 2 minutes. Remove the vinaigrette from heat and season to taste with salt and pepper. Stir in basil. Makes about 3 cups.

NOTES

Vinaigrettes can be made up to 2 hours in advance and left at room temperature. Sautéed Mushroom Vinaigrette can be made 1 day in advance. Refrigerate, covered, and rewarm over low heat before serving.

TRIED & TRUE

- Seed Crusted Salmon with Sautéed Mushroom Vinaigrette (page 151)
- Bruschetta Chicken with Two-Tomato Vinaigrette (page 172)
- Barcelona Chicken with Sautéed Mushroom Vinaigrette (page 173)
- Green Beans with Tomatoes & Feta (page 239)

SOMETHING NEW

- Use Two-Tomato Vinaigrette as a fresh, light sauce for pasta or as a topping for bruschetta.
- Spoon Sautéed Mushroom Vinaigrette over roasted asparagus or broccoli.
- Top sea bass, swordfish or halibut fillets with either vinaigrette.
- Top breaded pork chops with Sautéed Mushroom Vinaigrette.

Ginger–Lime Vinaigrette

1/4 CUP CHOPPED FRESH CILANTRO

1/4 CUP MINCED SCALLIONS

2 TABLESPOONS FRESH LIME JUICE

2 TABLESPOONS ASIAN SESAME OIL

2 TABLESPOONS UNSEASONED RICE VINEGAR

2 TABLESPOONS GRAPE SEED OIL OR OLIVE OIL

1/2 TABLESPOON THAI OR VIETNAMESE FISH SAUCE

2 TEASPOONS MINCED FRESH GINGER

1 TEASPOON MINCED FRESH GARLIC

1 TEASPOON GRATED LIME ZEST

1 TEASPOON DIJON MUSTARD

In a blender or mini-processor combine all ingredients. Purée. Refrigerate until needed, for up to 2 days. Makes about 3/4 cup.

Tried & True

- Sesame Seared Tuna Salad with Ginger-Lime Vinaigrette (page 159)
- Pac-Rim Mango Salad (page 225)

Something New

- Stir into steamed rice for a delicious Asian-flavored side dish.
- Toss with thinly sliced cucumbers and shredded carrots for a quick salad.
- Spoon over grilled or broiled shrimp for an easy appetizer.

MAPLE-MUSTARD GLAZE

$^{1}/_{4}$ CUP PURE MAPLE SYRUP

$^{1}/_{4}$ CUP GRAINY DIJON MUSTARD

2 TABLESPOONS BALSAMIC VINEGAR

$^{1}/_{4}$ TEASPOON CAYENNE PEPPER

Whisk together all ingredients. Makes about $^{2}/_{3}$ cup.

SPICED MAPLE-MUSTARD GLAZE

1 RECIPE MAPLE-MUSTARD GLAZE

$^{1}/_{2}$ TEASPOON GROUND GINGER

$^{1}/_{4}$ TEASPOON GROUND CINNAMON

Whisk together all ingredients. Makes about $^{2}/_{3}$ cup.

ASIAN MAPLE-MUSTARD GLAZE

$^{1}/_{4}$ CUP PURE MAPLE SYRUP

$^{1}/_{4}$ CUP GRAINY DIJON MUSTARD

$^{1}/_{4}$ CUP SOY SAUCE

2 TABLESPOONS UNSALTED BUTTER

2 TABLESPOONS MINCED GREEN ONION

1 TABLESPOON SESAME SEEDS

$^{1}/_{4}$ TEASPOON GROUND GINGER

In a small saucepan combine all ingredients and bring to a boil over medium heat, whisking to thoroughly incorporate butter. Simmer until syrupy, about 4 minutes. Makes about 1 cup.

HONEY-MUSTARD GLAZE

$^{1}/_{2}$ CUP HONEY

$^{1}/_{4}$ CUP SOY SAUCE

$^{1}/_{4}$ CUP DIJON MUSTARD

2 TABLESPOONS UNSALTED BUTTER

In a small saucepan combine all ingredients and bring to a boil over medium heat, whisking to thoroughly incorporate butter. Remove from heat. Makes about 1 cup.

Notes

All of these glazes contain some form of sugar (maple syrup, honey, etc.). Not only does this make them delicious additions to seafood, poultry, meat, and more; it makes them burn easily. When using the glazes, it is best to apply them during the second half of grilling, broiling, or oven roasting and to watch carefully!

Tried & True

- Prosciutto & Shrimp Skewers with Maple-Mustard Glaze (page 131)
- 5-Spice Shrimp Skewers with Asian Maple-Mustard Glaze (page 131)
- Gruyère Stuffed Salmon Burgers with Maple-Mustard Glaze (page 152)

Something New

- Brush any of the glazes over salmon fillets, chicken pieces, pork chops or scallops during grilling or broiling.
- Try any of the glazes on oven-roasted game hens or pork loin.
- Try Spiced Maple-Mustard Glaze on clove-studded ham.
- Drizzle Asian Maple Mustard Glaze over pan-seared duck breasts, dusted with Chinese 5-Spice Rub (page 36)

Honey-Rum Glaze

1/4	CUP DARK RUM	1	TABLESPOON DIJON MUSTARD
3	TABLESPOONS HONEY	1	TEASPOON GROUND ALLSPICE
2	TABLESPOONS BUTTER		SEA SALT AND FRESHLY GROUND PEPPER
2	TABLESPOONS JUICE PLUS GRATED ZEST FROM 1 LIME		

In a small saucepan combine the rum, honey, butter, lime juice and zest, mustard, and allspice. Bring to a boil over medium heat, whisking to incorporate the butter; boil gently until syrupy, about 4 minutes. Remove from the heat and season to taste with salt and pepper. Makes about 2/3 cup.

Pineapple-Rum Glaze

3	TABLESPOONS UNSALTED BUTTER	1/4	CUP DARK RUM
1	TEASPOON MINCED FRESH GARLIC	1/4	CUP DARK BROWN SUGAR
1	TEASPOON MINCED FRESH GINGER	2	MINCED SCALLIONS
1/4	CUP PINEAPPLE JUICE	1	TABLESPOON SOY SAUCE

In a small saucepan heat the butter over medium heat. Add the garlic and ginger and sauté for 2 minutes. Add the pineapple juice, rum, and brown sugar. Bring to a boil, whisking to dissolve the sugar and boil for 4 minutes. Add the scallions and soy sauce and boil for an additional 4 minutes or until syrupy. Remove from the heat. Makes about 3/4 cup.

Pineapple-Chile Glaze

3	tablespoons pineapple preserves	1½	tablespoon unsalted butter
3	tablespoons Thai-style sweet chile sauce	1	tablespoon fresh lime juice
		2	teaspoons soy sauce

In a small saucepan combine all ingredients. Bring to a boil over medium heat and boil for 2 minutes, stirring constantly. Remove from the heat. Makes about ½ cup.

Notes

All of these glazes contain some form of sugar (maple syrup, honey, etc.). Not only does this make them delicious additions to seafood, poultry, meat, and more; it makes them burn easily. When using the glazes, it is best to apply them during the second half of grilling, broiling, or oven roasting and to watch carefully!

Tried & True

- Caribbean Shrimp Skewers (page 131)
- Citrus Shrimp Skewers with Pineapple-Chile Glaze (page 131)

Something New

- Try them all on chicken, pork chops, salmon, tuna, scallops, or shrimp.
- Brush Honey-Rum Glaze over pineapple wedges during grilling.
- Wrap peach or apricot wedges in bacon; skewer and grill, brushing with Honey-Rum Glaze.

BOURBON-MOLASSES GLAZE

$1/4$ CUP BOURBON

$1/4$ CUP LIGHT MOLASSES

$1/4$ CUP BALSAMIC VINEGAR

$1/4$ CUP OLIVE OIL

In a small saucepan combine all ingredients and bring to a boil over medium heat. Boil for 10 minutes, whisking occasionally. Makes about $2/3$ cup.

ORANGE-BOURBON GLAZE

$1/4$ CUP UNSALTED BUTTER

$1/4$ CUP ORANGE MARMALADE

2   TABLESPOONS BOURBON

1   TABLESPOON GRAINY DIJON MUSTARD

1   TABLESPOON SOY SAUCE

1   TABLESPOON HONEY

1   TEASPOON MINCED FRESH GARLIC

In a small saucepan combine all ingredients and bring to a boil over medium heat. Boil for 4 minutes, whisking frequently. Makes about $3/4$ cup.

ORANGE-HOISIN GLAZE

$1/4$ CUP HOISIN SAUCE

2   TABLESPOONS FROZEN ORANGE JUICE CONCENTRATE, THAWED

1   TABLESPOON SOY SAUCE

2   GARLIC CLOVES, PRESSED

1   TEASPOON FRESHLY GRATED GINGER

1   TEASPOON RICE VINEGAR

In a small bowl combine all ingredients. Whisk thoroughly. Makes about $1/2$ cup.

NOTES

All of these glazes contain some form of sugar (maple syrup, honey, etc.). Not only does this make them delicious additions to seafood, poultry, meat, and more; it makes them burn easily. When using the glazes, it is best to apply them during the second half of grilling, broiling, or oven roasting and to watch carefully!

TRIED & TRUE

- Orange-Hoisin Shrimp Skewers (page 131)
- Orange-Bourbon Grilled Salmon (page 155)
- Bourbon-Molasses Rib-Eyes with Smoky Chipotle Butter (page 201)

SOMETHING NEW

- Brush Molasses-Bourbon Glaze on grilled hamburgers, pork chops, or steaks.
- Brush Orange-Bourbon Glaze over acorn squash rings during oven roasting.
- Try Orange-Hoisin Glaze on grilled tuna steaks or chicken breasts. Sprinkle with Sesame-Scallion Gremolata (page 88)

Mojito Glaze

Mojitos, the classic Cuban cocktail, are all the rage at restaurants and clubs and are one of my favorite ways to kick off summertime parties. This glaze has all of the flavors of the cocktail, plus a little kick from the jalapeños. Just for fun, I've included a recipe for Mojitos too!

$1/4$	CUP SPICED RUM (OR DARK RUM)	2	TABLESPOONS HONEY
$1/4$	CUP MINT JELLY	1	TABLESPOON DIJON MUSTARD
2	SMALL JALAPEÑO PEPPERS, SEEDED AND MINCED	1	TABLESPOON BUTTER
2	TABLESPOONS FRESH LIME JUICE PLUS GRATED ZEST FROM 1 LIME		

In a small saucepan combine all ingredients. Bring to a boil, whisking to dissolve the jelly. Boil gently, whisking occasionally, until reduced to a glaze, about 6 to 7 minutes. Remove from heat. Makes about $3/4$ cup.

Mojitos for a Crowd

2	CUPS PACKED FRESH MINT LEAVES	3	CUPS LIGHT RUM
1	CUP SUGAR	3	CUPS CLUB SODA
1	CUP FRESHLY SQUEEZED LIME JUICE		

Mash together mint, sugar, and lime juice and let stand for 30 minutes. Add rum and stir until sugar has completely dissolved.

Divide mixture among 12 tall glasses. Fill with ice. Top off with club soda and stir to combine. Sugar cane swizzle sticks make a great finishing touch!

Notes

Mojito Glaze can be made up to two days in advance. Cool, cover, and refrigerate.

Tried & True

Grilled Shrimp Skewers with Mojito Glaze (page 130)

Something New

Brush on chicken breasts, lamb chops or lamb kabobs during grilling.

PART TWO

APPETIZERS AND HORS D'OEUVRES

You'll find that the recipes in this section have flavors that really explode. Since people eat appetizers and hors d'oeuvres in small amounts, I like to make up for it with big flavors.

Many of the recipes can be either partially or fully prepared in advance, so make a variety of these tasty dishes for your next big party!

GRILLED SHRIMP SKEWERS WITH MOJITO GLAZE

Shrimp sizzling on the grill is a sure sign of a summer party in full swing! Don't forget to whip up a batch of Mojitos! The recipe's on page 124.

MARINADE

- 1/4 CUP FRESH LEMON JUICE
- 1/4 CUP OLIVE OIL
- 2 TABLESPOONS MINCED FRESH GARLIC
- 1 1/2 POUNDS MEDIUM PEELED AND DEVEINED SHRIMP

MOJITO GLAZE

- 1/4 CUP SPICED RUM (OR DARK RUM)
- 1/4 CUP MINT JELLY
- 2 SMALL JALAPEÑO PEPPERS, MINCED
- 2 TABLESPOONS FRESH LIME JUICE PLUS GRATED ZEST FROM 1 LIME
- 2 TABLESPOONS HONEY
- 1 TABLESPOON DIJON MUSTARD
- 1 TABLESPOON BUTTER
- 1/2 CUP PACKED FRESH MINT LEAVES
- SEA SALT AND FRESHLY GROUND PEPPER TO TASTE
- MINT SPRIGS FOR GARNISH (OPTIONAL)

Soak 8 long bamboo skewers in water for at least 30 minutes.

In a medium bowl whisk together the lemon juice, olive oil, and garlic. Add the shrimp and marinate for 30 to 45 minutes.

Meanwhile, in a small saucepan combine the rum, mint jelly, jalapeños, lime juice and zest, honey, mustard, and butter. Bring to a boil, whisking to dissolve the jelly. Boil gently, whisking occasionally, until reduced to a glaze, about 6 to 7 minutes. Remove from the heat.

Preheat the grill to medium-high heat.

Remove the shrimp from the marinade. Thread the shrimp and mint leaves onto skewers, separating each shrimp with 2 mint leaves. Sprinkle the skewers generously with salt and pepper. Grill, basting frequently with the glaze, until the shrimp is cooked throughout, about 5 minutes.

Place the skewers on a serving platter and garnish with mint sprigs if desired. Serves 8.

NOTES

Skewers may also be broiled. Watch carefully to ensure that glaze doesn't burn.

CLASSIC COMBOS

Island Teriyaki Shrimp Skewers
- *Replace marinade with Island Teriyaki Marinade (page 16).*
- *After removing shrimp, boil marinade for 3 minutes and use as glaze.*
- *Proceed as above, replacing mint leaves with pineapple chunks.*

Prosciutto & Shrimp Skewers
- *After removing shrimp from marinade above, wrap with thinly sliced prosciutto and thread onto skewers, omitting mint leaves.*
- *Proceed as above, replacing glaze with Maple-Mustard Glaze or Honey-Mustard Glaze (page 118).*

DARING PAIRINGS

5-Spice Shrimp Skewers with Asian Maple-Mustard Glaze
- *Replace marinade with Chinese 5-Spice Rub (page 36).*
- *Replace glaze with Asian Maple-Mustard Glaze (page 118).*
- *Omit mint leaves.*

Caribbean Shrimp Skewers
- *Replace marinade with Caribbean Rub (page 36).*
- *Replace glaze with Pineapple-Rum Glaze or Honey-Rum Glaze (page 120).*
- *Replace mint leaves with pineapple chunks.*

Citrus Shrimp Skewers with Pineapple-Chile Glaze
- *Replace half of the lemon juice in the marinade with lime juice.*
- *Replace glaze with Pineapple-Chile Glaze (page 121).*
- *Omit mint leaves.*

Orange-Hoisin Shrimp Skewers
- *Replace lemon juice in marinade with orange juice.*
- *Replace glaze with Orange-Hoisin Glaze (page 122).*
- *Omit mint leaves.*

CARIBBEAN SHRIMP COCKTAIL

I like to serve these festive shrimp appetizers in margarita or martini glasses garnished with lime wedges. The shrimp and salsas can be made a couple of hours in advance and refrigerated separately.

1   CUP DRY WHITE WINE

2   CELERY STALKS, CUT INTO 2-INCH LENGTHS

1   HANDFUL PARSLEY SPRIGS

1   TEASPOON BLACK PEPPERCORNS

1   GARLIC CLOVE, HALVED

1 1/2 POUNDS MEDIUM SHRIMP, PEELED AND DEVEINED

SAVORY CARIBBEAN SALSA

1   TABLESPOON OLIVE OIL

3/4 CUP MINCED SWEET ONION

2   TABLESPOONS SEEDED, MINCED JALAPEÑO PEPPER

1   TEASPOON MINCED GARLIC

1   TEASPOON GROUND CUMIN

1/4 TEASPOON GROUND ALLSPICE

1   CUP DICED FRESH PINEAPPLE

1/2 CUP PEELED, DICED MANGO

1/2 CUP PEELED, DICED PAPAYA

1   CUP QUARTERED CHERRY TOMATOES

1/2 CUP CHOPPED ROASTED RED PEPPERS (PAGE 9 OR STORE-BOUGHT)

1/4 CUP MINCED FRESH CILANTRO

2   TABLESPOONS FRESH LIME JUICE

SEA SALT AND FRESHLY CRACKED PEPPER TO TASTE

HABANERO HOT SAUCE (SUCH AS MELINDA'S) TO TASTE

In a large saucepan place the wine, celery, parsley, peppercorns, and halved garlic clove. Add water to fill halfway. Bring to a boil. Add the shrimp and simmer until cooked through, about 3 minutes. Drain the shrimp and rinse briefly with cold water. Cover and chill.

Meanwhile, in a medium skillet heat the oil over medium heat. Add the onion and sauté for 3 minutes. Add the jalapeño, garlic, cumin, and allspice, and sauté for 3 minutes. Stir in the pineapple, mango, papaya, tomatoes, and red peppers, and sauté for 2 more minutes. Remove from the heat and stir in the cilantro and lime juice. Season to taste with salt, pepper, and hot sauce. Cool to room temperature.

In a large bowl, stir together the shrimp and salsa and season to taste with salt and pepper. Divide between 6 dishes. Serves 6.

Classic Combos

Floribbean Shrimp Cocktail
Replace salsa with Floribbean Grilled Salsa (page 68).

Guacamole Shrimp Cocktail
- *Replace salsa with Guacamole (page 63).*
- *Top each serving with a dollop of cocktail sauce if desired. This variation is best served shortly after the guacamole is made.*

Daring Pairings

Greek Shrimp Cocktail
- *Replace salsa with 3 cups Greek Salsa (page 72).*
- *Garnish with lemon wedges.*

Pac-Rim Shrimp Cocktail
Replace salsa with Cucumber-Pineapple Salsa (page 66) mixed with 2 to 3 tablespoons bottled teriyaki sauce.

Garlic Lover's Steamed Mussels

Steamed mussels make an easy and impressive starter for a dinner party. You can tailor the flavors to fit perfectly with any dinner theme. Once you try a couple of my variations, I'm sure you'll come up with ideas of your own! Be sure to serve plenty of warm crusty bread alongside, to sop up the flavorful juices.

2	TABLESPOONS UNSALTED BUTTER	1¼	CUPS DRY WHITE WINE
2	TABLESPOONS EXTRA VIRGIN OLIVE OIL	3	POUNDS MUSSELS, SCRUBBED AND DEBEARDED
1	MEDIUM LEEK, CHOPPED, WHITE AND LIGHT GREEN PARTS ONLY	1	TABLESPOON ROASTED GARLIC (PAGE 8 OR STORE-BOUGHT)
4	GARLIC CLOVES, MINCED	¼	CUP CHOPPED ITALIAN PARSLEY
¼	CUP DICED CELERY		
	SEA SALT AND FRESHLY GROUND PEPPER		

In a large pot melt the butter in oil over medium heat. Add the leek, garlic, and celery. Sprinkle generously with salt and pepper and sauté until the vegetables are tender, about 7 minutes. Add the wine and bring to a boil. Add the mussels, cover, and cook until they open, about 7 minutes.

Remove the pot from the heat. Remove the mussels to a large serving bowl with a slotted spoon, discarding any that did not open. Whisk the roasted garlic into the wine mixture remaining in the pot and pour over the mussels. Sprinkle with parsley and serve. Serves 6.

Classic Combos

Mussels Provençal
- *Add 1 chopped fennel bulb along with leek, garlic and celery.*
- *Add 1 bay leaf and 1/4 cup Pernod, or other anise flavored liqueur, along with wine.*
- *Omit roasted garlic.*

Coconut-Curry Mussels
- *Replace leek with 1 bunch thinly sliced scallions.*
- *Add 1 tablespoon minced fresh ginger along with scallions and garlic.*
- *Omit celery, sea salt, and pepper.*
- *Add 1 tablespoon Thai green or red curry paste to sautéed scallion mixture and cook for 1 minute, prior to adding liquids.*
- *Replace wine with 1 cup canned coconut milk and 2 tablespoons Asian fish sauce.*

- *Omit roasted garlic.*
- *Replace parsley with cilantro.*
- *Squeeze 1 to 2 tablespoons fresh lime juice over finished dish.*

Mussels Marinara

- *Reduce white wine to $1/2$ cup and add 1 cup Red Wine Marinara (page 100) or your favorite store-bought brand.*
- *Omit roasted garlic.*
- *Replace parsley with julienned fresh basil.*

DARING PAIRINGS

Mussels Mexicano

- *Replace leek with 1 bunch thinly sliced scallions.*
- *Add 1 to 2 seeded, minced jalapeño peppers and 1 cup chopped tomatoes along with scallions, garlic and celery.*
- *Replace wine with $3/4$ cup chicken broth and $1/4$ cup tequila.*
- *Omit roasted garlic.*
- *Replace parsley with cilantro.*
- *Squeeze 1 to 2 tablespoons fresh lime juice over finished dish.*

Smoky Spanish Mussels

- *Add 3 ounces chopped, fully cooked Chorizo sausage and 1 teaspoon Spanish smoked paprika (pimentón) along with leeks and garlic.*
- *Replace celery with green bell pepper.*
- *Replace wine with dry (Fino) sherry.*
- *Replace roasted garlic with 2 tablespoons good quality sherry vinegar.*

Chicken-Chorizo Skewers with Roasted Garlic & Red Pepper Aioli

These spicy skewers would make a great starter for an outdoor BBQ, but would also make a substantial entrée for 4, served with some grilled baby potatoes. Toss the potatoes with the same spice mixture as the chicken! Serve the Thai variation on a bed of coconut-pineapple rice.

Roasted Garlic & Red Pepper Aioli

$1/2$ cup mayonnaise

$1/2$ cup chopped roasted red peppers (page 9 or store-bought)

1 medium shallot, chopped

1 tablespoon roasted garlic (page 8 or store-bought)

$1/2$ tablespoons Worcestershire sauce
A few dashes hot sauce (optional)
Salt and pepper to taste

Chicken-Chorizo Skewers

12 ounces boneless, skinless chicken breasts, cut into 1-inch pieces

1 teaspoon ground coriander

$1/2$ teaspoons ground cumin

$1/2$ teaspoons smoked paprika

12 ounces fully cooked chorizo sausages, sliced $1/2$-inch thick

1 red onion, cut into 1-inch pieces
Sea salt and freshly ground pepper
Vegetable oil or nonstick cooking spray

2 tablespoons chopped fresh Italian parsley, plus sprigs for garnish

Soak 8 to 10 long bamboo skewers in water for at least 30 minutes, or set aside 8 to 10 metal skewers. Preheat grill to medium-high heat.

In a blender or mini-processor combine the mayonnaise, peppers, shallot, and Worcestershire, and purée. Season to taste with hot sauce, salt, and pepper. Cover and refrigerate until needed, up to 2 days.

Sprinkle the chicken pieces with coriander, cumin, and paprika. Thread the chicken, chorizo, and onion pieces alternately onto the prepared skewers. Brush or spray with oil and sprinkle with salt and pepper. Grill until the chicken pieces are cooked through, about 8 minutes, turning frequently.

Remove the skewers to a platter; drizzle with a little of the aioli and sprinkle with parsley. Garnish with parsley sprigs if desired. Serve remaining aioli in a bowl alongside. Serves 8 to 10.

NOTES

- Skewers can also be broiled.
- Substitute trimmed chicken thigh meat if desired.

CLASSIC COMBO

Thai Coconut Chicken Sate with Spicy Peanut Dipping Sauce
- *Replace aioli with Spicy Peanut Dipping Sauce (page 60) at room temperature.*
- *Marinate chicken chunks in Thai Coconut Marinade (page 14) for 2 to 4 hours before grilling.*
- *Omit spices, chorizo, onion, and parsley.*

DARING PAIRINGS

Cajun Chicken & Andouille Skewers with Remoulade
- *Replace aioli with Roasted Red Pepper Remoulade (page 50).*
- *Replace coriander, cumin and paprika with 1½ tablespoons Cajun-Creole Spice Rub (page 34) or store-bought.*
- *Replace chorizo with fully cooked Andouille sausages.*
- *Replace onion with green bell pepper chunks.*
- **If using a purchased Cajun-Creole spice blend, check the salt level and package directions and adjust accordingly.*

Chimichurri Chicken Skewers
- *Replace aioli with Chimichurri Sauce (page 104).*
- *Replace coriander, cumin, and paprika with 1½ tablespoons Southwest Spice Rub (page 34) or store-bought.*
- *If you are using a purchased Southwest spice blend, check the salt level and package directions and adjust accordingly.*

CROSTINI WITH GOAT CHEESE & ROASTED EGGPLANT-PEPPER TAPENADE

ROASTED EGGPLANT-PEPPER TAPENADE

1 MEDIUM EGGPLANT, UNPEELED AND CUT INTO $1/2$-INCH CHUNKS (ABOUT 4 CUPS)

1 MEDIUM RED BELL PEPPER, CUT INTO $1/2$-INCH CHUNKS

1 MEDIUM YELLOW BELL PEPPER, CUT INTO $1/2$-INCH CHUNKS

1 LARGE SWEET ONION, CUT INTO $1/2$-INCH CHUNKS

$1/4$ CUP EXTRA VIRGIN OLIVE OIL
    SEA SALT AND FRESHLY GROUND PEPPER

$1/2$ CUP PITTED, CHOPPED KALAMATA OR GAETA OLIVES

2 TABLESPOONS DRAINED, MINCED CAPERS

$1^1/2$ TABLESPOONS GOOD BALSAMIC VINEGAR

$1^1/2$ TABLESPOONS BASIL-MINT PESTO (PAGE 104 OR STORE-BOUGHT BASIL PESTO)

1 TABLESPOON ROASTED GARLIC (PAGE 8 OR STORE-BOUGHT)

24 $1/2$-INCH THICK DIAGONAL BAGUETTE SLICES

2 TO 3 TABLESPOONS EXTRA VIRGIN OLIVE OIL

5 TO 6 OUNCES SOFT, FRESH GOAT CHEESE

Preheat the oven to 425°.

On a large, heavy baking sheet or roasting pan drizzle the eggplant, bell peppers, and onion with olive oil and toss well to coat evenly. Sprinkle generously with salt and pepper. Roast in the center of the oven for 20 minutes. Remove the pan, stir, return to the oven, and roast for an additional 20 minutes or until the vegetables are soft and beginning to brown.

Remove the mixture to a large bowl and mash lightly with a potato masher. Stir in the olives, capers, balsamic vinegar, pesto, and garlic.

Reduce the oven temperature to 375°.

Brush both sides of the bread slices lightly with olive oil and place on a large baking sheet. Bake in the middle of the oven until lightly toasted, about 10 minutes.

Spread the crostini with goat cheese and top with tapenade. Makes 24.

NOTES

Crostini can be baked one day ahead and stored, airtight, at room temperature. Tapenade can be made 3 days ahead, covered, and refrigerated. Bring to room temperature before using.

CLASSIC COMBOS

Crostini with Goat Cheese & Wild Mushrooms
> *Replace tapenade with Wild Mushroom Sauté (page 86).*

Crostini with Brie & Chutney
- *Replace tapenade with Spiced Apple-Pear Chutney (page 74).*
- *Replace goat cheese with Brie or Camembert cheese.*

DARING PAIRINGS

Crostini with Gorgonzola & Onion Jam
- *Replace tapenade with Sweet & Savory Onion Jam (page 78).*
- *Replace goat cheese with Gorgonzola or other creamy blue cheese.*

Crostini with Feta & Greek Salsa
- *Replace tapenade with Greek Salsa (page 72).*
- *Mix an additional ½ cup feta into salsa.*
- *Omit goat cheese.*
- *Salsa is best served in a bowl alongside the crostini, so they stay crisp.*

Crostini with Queso Fresco and Charred Pepper & Onion Relish
- *Replace tapenade with Charred Pepper & Onion Relish (page 84), mixed with 1 cup crumbled queso fresco cheese.*
- *Omit goat cheese.*

CHUTNEY STUFFED BRIE EN CROUTE

ROSEMARY–DRIED FRUIT CHUTNEY

- $3/4$ CUP DRIED CRANBERRIES
- $3/4$ CUP DRIED CHERRIES
- $3/4$ CUP CHOPPED DRIED FIGS
- 1 LARGE RED ONION, CHOPPED
- $3/4$ CUP WATER
- $3/4$ CUP CIDER VINEGAR
- $2/3$ CUP PACKED LIGHT BROWN SUGAR
- 2 TABLESPOONS MINCED FRESH ROSEMARY
- 1 TABLESPOON MINCED FRESH GARLIC
- 1 TEASPOON GRATED ZEST PLUS $1/4$ CUP JUICE FROM 1 ORANGE
- 1 TEASPOON GRATED ZEST PLUS 1

- TABLESPOON JUICE FROM 1 LEMON
- 1 TEASPOON SEA SALT
- $1/2$ TEASPOON CAYENNE PEPPER
- $2/3$ CUP SLIVERED ALMONDS, LIGHTLY TOASTED
- $1^1/2$ CUPS CHOPPED DRIED APRICOTS

- 2 $17^1/4$-OUNCE PACKAGES FROZEN PUFF PASTRY, THAWED ACCORDING TO PACKAGE DIRECTIONS.
- 2 15- TO 17-OUNCE WHEELS OF BRIE CHEESE, CHILLED
- 2 LARGE EGGS, LIGHTLY BEATEN

In a large, non-reactive saucepan combine the cranberries, cherries, figs, onion, water, cider vinegar, brown sugar, rosemary, garlic, orange zest and juice, lemon zest and juice, salt, cayenne pepper, and almonds. Heat the mixture over medium-high heat and bring to a boil, stirring to dissolve the sugar. Reduce the heat and simmer until the fruit and onion are soft and the chutney is thick, about 40 minutes. Stir in the apricots. Cool to room temperature.

Roll out one sheet of pastry into a 13-inch square and cut out a round the size of the Brie. Use the scraps for decorative cutouts if desired. Roll out a second sheet of pastry into a 13-inch square and transfer to a baking sheet. Cut the Brie in half horizontally and place one half, cut side up, on pastry square. Spread one cup of the chutney on the Brie half and place the other half on top, cut side down.

Wrap the pastry tightly over the Brie, trimming the excess and leaving about a 1-inch border. Brush egg lightly over the border and place the other pastry circle on top, pressing to seal.

Flip the stuffed Brie over, so the smooth side is on top. Brush the top and sides lightly with egg. Place any decorative cutouts on top and brush, tops only, with egg (the cutouts won't rise if egg drips down the sides.) Repeat the entire process to make 2 stuffed Brie rounds. Place a couple of inches apart on baking sheet and chill, uncovered for 30 minutes.

Preheat the oven to 425°. Bake for about 20 minutes or until the pastry is puffed and golden. Let stand for 15 minutes. Serve with crackers or baguette slices. Serves 20.

NOTES

- You will have leftover chutney. Chill, airtight, for up to 2 months.
- Brie can be stuffed and wrapped 1 day in advance. Cover with plastic wrap and refrigerate. Wait until 30 minutes before baking to brush with egg.

CLASSIC COMBO

Raspberry Stuffed Brie en Croute
Replace the chutney with an equal amount of raspberry jam or preserves.

DARING PAIRING

Wild Mushroom Stuffed Brie en Croute
Replace the chutney with Wild Mushroom Sauté (page 86), made without the cream.

Herbed Smoked Salmon & Prosciutto Pinwheels

Perfect for parties, these tasty hors d'oeuvres can be prepared up to 3 days in advance. Just slice and bake while your guests are on their way. The smoked salmon version here is particularly good with Champagne!

1	SHEET FROZEN PUFF PASTRY (HALF OF A 17-OUNCE PACKAGE), THAWED	2	TABLESPOONS DRAINED, CHOPPED CAPERS
3	OUNCES THINLY SLICED PROSCIUTTO HAM	1	TABLESPOON CHOPPED FRESH DILL
6	OUNCES CHIVE & ONION CREAM CHEESE SPREAD	1	TEASPOON MINCED FRESH LEMON ZEST
3	OUNCES SMOKED SALMON (LOX-STYLE), CHOPPED	1	EGG, LIGHTLY BEATEN

Place the pastry sheet on your work surface. Cut in half, forming two 9$^1/_2$ x 4$^3/_4$-inch rectangles. Arrange half of the prosciutto on 1 rectangle, leaving a $^1/_2$-inch border along one long side.

Spread half of the cheese evenly over the prosciutto. Sprinkle half of each: salmon, capers, dill, and lemon zest over the cream cheese.

Brush the plain border with egg. Starting at the long side opposite the border, roll up the pastry, jelly-roll style, pressing gently to seal along the long edge. Wrap tightly in plastic. Repeat with the remaining ingredients to form a second log. Refrigerate at least 3 hours and up to 3 days.

Preheat the oven to 400°. Line a large baking sheet with parchment paper.

Cut the logs crosswise into $^1/_2$-inch-thick pinwheels. Arrange the pinwheels on the prepared baking sheet, spacing about 1 inch apart. Bake until pastry is golden brown, about 20 minutes. Transfer to racks to cool slightly. Serve warm. Makes 36.

NOTES

For all of the variations below, omit the cream cheese, salmon, capers, dill, and lemon zest. Top the prosciutto layer with the ingredients below, in the order listed, and proceed with the recipe as directed above. Quantities below are for the full recipe.

CLASSIC COMBOS

Pesto, Parmesan & Pine Nut Pinwheels
- *¼ cup pesto (page 104 or store-bought)*
- *¼ cup toasted pine nuts*
- *1½ cups freshly grated Parmesan*

Wild Mushroom & Gruyère Pinwheels
- *6 ounces wild mushrooms, such as cremini, shiitake and chanterelle, sautéed in a little butter or olive oil*
- *1 tablespoon minced fresh thyme*
- *1 cup freshly shredded Gruyère cheese*

DARING PAIRINGS

Cranberry, Pecan & Blue Cheese Pinwheels
- *½ cup dried cranberries*
- *½ cup crumbled blue cheese*
- *¼ cup toasted, chopped pecans*

Shrimp, Feta & Sun-Dried Tomato Pinwheels
- *3 ounces chopped, cooked shrimp*
- *½ cup crumbled feta cheese*
- *½ cup minced, oil-packed sun-dried tomatoes, drained*

Polynesian Pinwheels
- *6 ounces pineapple cream cheese spread*
- *3 ounces chopped cooked shrimp or ham*
- *¼ cup chopped, salted cashews*

CARAMELIZED LEEK, MUSHROOM & SUN-DRIED TOMATO CHEESECAKE

This savory cheesecake has been the runaway hit of many cocktail parties! It is very rich and is best served spread on warm baguette slices. Either cut it into thin wedges for a sit-down appetizer or leave it whole, on a pretty cake stand, surrounded by the baguette slices, as part of an hors d'oeuvres buffet.

2 CUPS BREADCRUMBS MADE FROM CRUSTLESS FRENCH BREAD

5 TABLESPOONS BUTTER, MELTED

1 8.5-OUNCE JAR OIL-PACKED SUN-DRIED TOMATOES, DRAINED, CHOPPED, OIL RESERVED

2 LARGE LEEKS, HALVED LENGTHWISE AND THINLY SLICED, WHITE AND LIGHT GREEN PARTS ONLY (ABOUT 4 CUPS)

18 OUNCES CREMINI MUSHROOMS, HALVED AND THINLY SLICED

1 TEASPOON MINCED FRESH GARLIC

1½ TEASPOONS SEA SALT, DIVIDED

3 8-OUNCE PACKAGES CREAM CHEESE, SOFTENED

1 TABLESPOON ROASTED GARLIC (PAGE 8 OR STORE-BOUGHT)

3 EGGS

2 CRUSTY BAGUETTES, SLICED

Preheat the oven to 350°.

In a medium bowl toss together the breadcrumbs and melted butter and press the mixture into the bottom of a 9-inch springform pan. Bake the crust for 10 minutes or until golden. Cool while preparing filling. Maintain oven temperature.

In a large nonstick skillet heat 1½ tablespoons reserved sun-dried tomato oil over medium heat. Add the leeks and sauté until golden and soft, about 15 minutes. Remove the leeks to a medium bowl.

Wipe out the skillet. Place over medium-high heat and add 1½ tablespoons sun-dried tomato oil. Add the mushrooms and sauté until the liquid they release has evaporated and the mushrooms are beginning to brown, about 10 minutes, adding minced garlic during the last 2 minutes. Add to the bowl with the leeks and mix in ½ teaspoon sea salt. Set aside to cool slightly.

In a large bowl beat the cream cheese, roasted garlic, and remaining 1 teaspoon sea salt until fluffy. Beat in the eggs, one at a time, just until blended. Stir in the sun-dried tomatoes.

Pour half of the cream cheese mixture into the prepared crust. Scatter the mushroom mixture evenly over, then cover with the remaining cream cheese mixture. Bake for 50 minutes, or until lightly browned. It should be set around the edges and just slightly wobbly in the center. Cool to room temperature, or at least 1 hour. Carefully remove the sides of the springform pan and transfer the cake to a platter or plates. Serves 16 to 24.

NOTES

To make removal of the cake to a platter easier, line the bottom of your springform pan with parchment paper.

CLASSIC COMBO

Savory Tuscan Cheesecake
- *Replace sun-dried tomato oil with extra virgin olive oil.*
- *Add 1 cup freshly grated Parmesan cheese to bowl with leek/mushroom mixture after cooling.*
- *Replace roasted garlic with 2 tablespoons pesto (page 104 or store-bought).*
- *Replace sun-dried tomatoes with 1 cup lightly toasted pine nuts.*

DARING PAIRINGS

Caramelized Leek, Mushroom & Cranberry Cheesecake
- *Replace sun-dried tomato oil with extra virgin olive oil.*
- *Saute 3 ounces chopped pancetta with the leeks.*
- *Omit roasted garlic.*
- *Replace sun-dried tomatoes with 1 cup dried cranberries that have been soaked in hot water or wine for 20 minutes, drained and patted dry.*

Tapenade Filled Cheesecake
- *Omit reserved sun-dried tomato oil, leeks, mushrooms, minced garlic, and roasted garlic.*
- *Replace leek/mushroom layer with 1 recipe Roasted Eggplant-Pepper Tapenade (page 80).*

Moroccan Chicken Phyllo Triangles

These tasty triangles are fun to make and even more fun to eat. Make a couple of batches on a lazy Sunday afternoon and keep them in the freezer, to pull out for unexpected guests.

1/4 CUP OLIVE OIL	1 POUND GROUND CHICKEN
1 BUNCH SCALLIONS, MINCED	SEA SALT AND FRESHLY GROUND PEPPER
2 TABLESPOONS MINCED FRESH GINGER	3/4 CUP CHOPPED DRIED APRICOTS
1 TABLESPOON MINCED GARLIC	8 OUNCES CREAM CHEESE, SOFTENED
1 TEASPOON GROUND CUMIN	1/2 CUP UNSALTED BUTTER, MELTED
1 TEASPOON GROUND CINNAMON	16 PHYLLO SHEETS (14 x 18 INCHES) THAWED, PLUS EXTRA AS BACKUP
1/2 TEASPOON GROUND CORIANDER	ITALIAN PARSLEY OR CILANTRO SPRIGS FOR GARNISH (OPTIONAL)
1/4 TEASPOON GROUND TURMERIC (OPTIONAL)	

In a large skillet heat 2 tablespoons olive oil over medium-high heat. Add the scallions, ginger, and garlic and sauté for 3 minutes. Stir in the cumin, cinnamon, coriander, and turmeric and cook 1 minute. Add chicken to the skillet; sprinkle with salt and pepper and cook for 7 minutes, breaking up clumps, or until fully cooked and all liquid has evaporated. Remove the chicken mixture to a large bowl and stir in the apricots and cream cheese. Season with additional salt and pepper if desired and cool.

Preheat the oven to 400°. Cover 2 large baking sheets with parchment paper or lightly oil. Whisk the remaining 2 tablespoons olive oil into the melted butter. Place 1 phyllo sheet on your work surface, short edge facing you. Brush the sheet lightly with the melted butter mixture (keep the remaining phyllo covered with plastic wrap and a damp kitchen towel.) Top with a second phyllo sheet. Brush with butter. Cut the sheets lengthwise into 5 equal strips, trimming uneven edges as needed.

Place about 1 rounded tablespoon of the chicken mixture at the base of one strip. Fold one corner of the phyllo strip over filling. Repeat the folding down the length of the strip, as for a flag, forming a triangle. Brush any rough edges with butter and place on the prepared baking sheet. Repeat with the remaining phyllo sheets and filling.

Bake the triangles until golden brown, about 15 to 17 minutes. If baking on 2 oven racks, switch position of pans halfway through. Transfer to a platter, garnish with herb sprigs, and serve. Makes 40.

NOTES

Triangles can be prepared, but not baked, one day in advance and refrigerated in airtight containers or tightly wrapped and frozen for up to three months. Bake slightly longer if directly from chilled or frozen state.

CLASSIC COMBOS

Greek Pork Phyllo Triangles
- *Replace scallions with ½ cup minced red onion.*
- *Omit ginger and increase garlic to 1½ tablespoons.*
- *Omit cumin, cinnamon, and turmeric.*
- *Increase coriander to 1½ teaspoons and add 2 teaspoons dried oregano, 2 teaspoons dried mint, and 1 teaspoon grated lemon zest at the same time.*
- *Replace ground chicken with ground pork.*
- *Replace cream cheese with feta cheese. Omit apricots.*
- *These would be great served with either of the tzatzikis on pages 76–77.*

Herbed Turkey & Cranberry Phyllo Triangles
- *Omit ginger.*
- *Replace spices (cumin, cinnamon, coriander, and turmeric) with 2 tablespoons chopped fresh sage, 2 tablespoons chopped fresh rosemary, 1 tablespoon chopped fresh thyme, and ½ teaspoon ground allspice.*
- *Replace ground chicken with ground turkey.*
- *Replace apricots with chopped dried cranberries.*

DARING PAIRINGS

Turkish Lamb Phyllo Triangles
- *Replace scallions with ½ cup minced red onion. Omit the ginger.*
- *Add 2 teaspoons Aleppo pepper flakes, 2 teaspoons dried mint, 1 teaspoon ground allspice, and ½ teaspoon ground sumac or grated lemon zest, along with cumin. Omit cinnamon, coriander, and turmeric.*
- *Replace ground chicken with ground lamb.*

Polynesian Pork & Pineapple Phyllo Triangles
- *Replace spices (cumin, cinnamon, coriander, and turmeric) with 2 teaspoons Chinese 5-spice powder plus 2 tablespoons soy sauce.*
- *Replace ground chicken with ground pork. Omit salt.*
- *Replace apricots with chopped dried pineapple.*

FISH

Fish is not only delicious and healthy, it adapts well to a wide variety of flavors and cooking methods. The recipes in this chapter incorporate many marinades, salsas, and sauces from Part One. Check out my combinations, then create some of your own!

I have included several salmon dishes because it is tasty, widely available, and economical. Although wild-caught fresh salmon is my preferred choice, all of these recipes are also delicious with farm-raised salmon.

Many of these recipes call for grilling, but for each I have given suggestions for indoor cooking methods. I live in Minnesota, so believe me when I say they've all been tested indoors!

Spice Dusted Salmon with Curried Orange-Apricot Sauce

This recipe is based on one that earned me the $10,000 Grand Prize at the 2004 Florida Citrus Cook-Off, sponsored by Florida's Natural Growers. The pink salmon, bright orange sauce and green cilantro make for a beautiful dinner party entrée, although the recipe is certainly easy enough for a weeknight meal. Couscous with dried fruit and almonds would be a terrific side!

Curried Orange-Apricot Sauce

- 2 TABLESPOONS OLIVE OIL
- 1/4 CUP MINCED SHALLOTS
- 1 TEASPOON CURRY POWDER
- 1 CUP FRESH ORANGE JUICE
- 1 CUP PLUS 1 TABLESPOON LOW SODIUM CHICKEN BROTH, DIVIDED
- 1/4 CUP APRICOT PRESERVES, LARGE APRICOT PIECES CHOPPED
- 1/8 TEASPOON CAYENNE PEPPER
- 1 1/2 TEASPOONS CORNSTARCH

Spice Mix

- 2 TEASPOONS GROUND CUMIN
- 2 TEASPOONS GROUND CORIANDER
- 1 TEASPOON SEA SALT
- 1/2 TEASPOON FRESHLY GROUND PEPPER

- 4 7-OUNCE CENTER-CUT SALMON FILLETS, SKINNED
- 1 TABLESPOON OLIVE OIL
- 2 TABLESPOONS CHOPPED FRESH CILANTRO
  CILANTRO SPRIGS FOR GARNISH

In a medium saucepan heat the olive oil over medium heat. Add the shallots and sauté for 3 minutes. Stir in the curry powder and cook for 1 minute. Add the orange juice and 1 cup of the chicken broth; increase the heat and boil until reduced by half, about 10 minutes. Reduce the heat to medium and whisk in the apricot preserves and cayenne. Whisk together the cornstarch and remaining 1 tablespoon chicken broth and whisk into the sauce. Cook for 2 minutes or until thick and bubbly. Keep warm over low heat.

In a small bowl mix together the cumin, coriander, salt, and pepper. Sprinkle the spice mixture over tops of salmon fillets. In a large nonstick skillet heat 1 tablespoon olive oil over medium-high heat. Add the salmon, spice side down, and cook for 4 minutes. Flip the salmon, lower the heat to medium, and continue to cook until just cooked through and no longer translucent in the center, about 6 minutes.

Place the salmon on a platter or plates, drizzle with sauce, and sprinkle with cilantro. Garnish with cilantro sprigs if desired. Pass the remaining sauce separately. Serves 4.

Classic Combo

Mustard Seed Salmon with Lemon-Dill Aioli
- *Replace sauce with Lemon-Dill Aioli (page 46).*
- *Replace spice mix with 2½ tablespoons Toasted Mustard Seed Crust (page 38).*
- *Omit cilantro.*
- *Garnish with dill sprigs and lemon wedges.*

Daring Pairings

Ancho-Spiced Salmon with Cherry Port Sauce
- *Replace sauce with Cherry-Port Sauce (page 92).*
- *Replace spice mix with 1 recipe Ancho-Cinnamon Spice Rub (page 36).*
- *Omit cilantro.*
- *Garnish with thyme sprigs.*

Seed Crusted Salmon with Orange Romesco Sauce.
- *Replace sauce with Orange Romesco Sauce (page 102).*
- *Replace spice mix with 1 recipe Mediterranean Seed Crust (page 38).*
- *Replace cilantro with Italian parsley.*

Seed Crusted Salmon with Sautéed Mushroom Vinaigrette
- *Replace sauce with Sautéed Mushroom Vinaigrette (page 114).*
- *Replace spice mix with 1 recipe Mediterranean Seed Crust (page 38).*
- *Replace cilantro with Italian parsley.*

GRUYÈRE STUFFED SALMON BURGERS WITH MAPLE-MUSTARD GLAZE

Gruyère is a slightly sweet and nutty cheese that melts beautifully. I love the flavor of it in these burgers, but you could substitute Provolone, Fontina, or smoked Gouda if preferred.

BURGERS

2 POUNDS SALMON FILLETS, SKINNED AND FINELY CHOPPED

2 OUNCES FINELY CHOPPED PANCETTA

2 TABLESPOONS HONEY DIJON MUSTARD

2 TABLESPOONS WORCESTERSHIRE SAUCE

1 TABLESPOON MINCED FRESH SAGE

1 TABLESPOON MINCED FRESH THYME

1 TEASPOON COARSE SEA SALT OR KOSHER SALT

$1/2$ TEASPOON FRESHLY GROUND PEPPER

$1^1/2$ CUPS PANKO

$1^1/2$ CUPS SHREDDED GRUYÈRE CHEESE

MAPLE-MUSTARD GLAZE

$1/2$ CUP PURE MAPLE SYRUP

$1/2$ CUP GRAINY DIJON MUSTARD

$1/4$ CUP BALSAMIC VINEGAR

$1/2$ TEASPOON CAYENNE PEPPER

$1/4$ CUP MAYONNAISE

6 $1/2$-INCH THICK RED ONION SLICES OLIVE OIL

6 KAISER ROLLS, OR OTHER BURGER BUNS

In a large bowl combine the chopped salmon with pancetta, mustard, Worcestershire, sage, thyme, salt, and pepper, and mix well. Thoroughly mix in the panko and form the mixture into 12 patties. Place 6 of the patties on the work surface and place a mound of cheese in the center of each. Cover with the remaining 6 patties and thoroughly seal the edges. Place the burgers on a plate and refrigerate for at least 30 minutes and up to 2 hours.

Preheat the grill to medium-high heat. In a medium bowl whisk together the glaze ingredients. Remove $1/4$ cup of glaze to a small bowl and whisk with the mayonnaise. Refrigerate the mayonnaise mixture until the burgers are ready to serve.

Slide the onion slices onto long metal skewers and brush with olive oil. Grill over direct heat for 2 minutes per side or until lightly charred. Move to a cooler part of the grill and continue to cook, basting frequently with the Maple-Mustard Glaze, until softened and lightly charred, about 10 more minutes.

Meanwhile, brush the salmon burgers with oil; place over direct heat and grill for 3 minutes. Carefully turn the burgers, brush tops with glaze, and grill for 3 more minutes. Turn the burgers again, brush with more glaze, and grill until cooked through, about 2 more minutes.

Remove the burgers and onions from the grill and toast the buns, cut sides down, along the outer edges of grill, about 1 to 2 minutes. Spread ½ tablespoon mayonnaise mixture on the bottom halves of buns; top with a burger, the remaining mayo mixture, and an onion slice. Serves 6

NOTES

Burgers can also be broiled.

CLASSIC COMBO

Gruyère Stuffed Salmon Burgers with Corn Salsa
- *Replace sage with 1 teaspoon dried oregano.*
- *Omit Maple-Mustard Glaze and red onions.*
- *Spread bottoms of buns with ½ tablespoon mayonnaise, omitting remaining mayonnaise.*
- *Spoon Pancetta-Corn Salsa (page 60) on bottoms of buns and atop burgers.*

DARING PAIRING

Blue Cheese Stuffed Salmon Burgers with Onion Jam & Wild Mushrooms
- *Omit glaze, mayonnaise and red onions.*
- *Replace sage with rosemary.*
- *Replace Gruyère with 4 ounces blue cheese, formed into disks, about 1½ inches in diameter.*
- *Spoon Wild Mushroom Sauté (page 86) on bottom of buns.*
- *Top burgers with Sweet & Savory Onion Jam (page 78).*
- *Use remaining Wild Mushroom Sauté for Wild Mushroom Smashed Potatoes (page 231) to serve alongside if desired.*

Miso Grilled Salmon with Sesame-Scallion Gremolata

This easy Japanese-flavored salmon is absolutely delicious! Perfect for a warm summer evening out on the deck. Toss some of the gremolata with steamed Jasmine rice or sprinkle over grilled asparagus spears to serve alongside.

Miso-Mustard Marinade

- $1/2$ cup light (Shiro) miso
- $1/2$ cup mirin
- $1/4$ cup sake
- 2 tablespoons sugar
- 1 tablespoon Chinese hot mustard (or other spicy mustard)

Sesame-Scallion Gremolata

- $1/2$ cup minced scallions, white and light green parts only
- $1^1/2$ tablespoons toasted sesame seeds
- 1 teaspoon minced fresh garlic
- 1 teaspoon grated fresh lime zest
- Sea salt to taste

- 4 center-cut salmon fillets, about 7 ounces each, skinned

In a small bowl whisk together the miso, mirin, sake, sugar, and mustard. Pour the marinade into a large, heavy duty ziplock bag. Add the salmon and place in the refrigerator for 2 to 3 hours. Turn the bag occasionally.

Meanwhile, make the gremolata. In a small bowl combine the scallions, sesame seeds, garlic, and lime zest in a small bowl. Season lightly with salt. Refrigerate until needed.

Preheat the grill to medium-high heat. Remove the fish from the marinade and discard the remaining marinade. Oil the grill or fish basket and grill the fish over direct heat until just cooked though, about 4 to 6 minutes per side.

Place the salmon on a platter or plates and sprinkle with gremolata. Serves 4.

NOTES

Salmon can also be broiled.

CLASSIC COMBOS

Mustard-Sage Grilled Salmon
- *Replace marinade with Mustard-Sage Marinade (page 28)*
- *Sprinkle salmon with salt and pepper after removing from marinade.*
- *Omit gremolata.*
- *Serve with Pancetta & Leek Mashed Potatoes (page 230) if desired.*

Southwest Grilled Salmon with Cilantro-Lime Butter
- *Omit marinade.*
- *Rub 2 teaspoons Southwest Spice Rub (page 34 or store-bought) plus $1/2$ tablespoon vegetable oil onto each salmon fillet before grilling.*
- *Top grilled salmon with $1/4$-inch thick slices of Cilantro-Lime Butter (page 56) and tent with foil for a few minutes before serving.*
- *This variation can also be pan-seared.*

DARING PAIRINGS

Orange-Sesame Grilled Salmon
- *Replace marinade with Orange-Sesame Teriyaki Marinade (page 16).*
- *After removing salmon from marinade, boil marinade in a small saucepan for 2–3 minutes and use to glaze salmon during second half of grilling.*
- *Gremolata is optional.*

Orange-Bourbon Grilled Salmon
- *Omit marinade.*
- *Rub salmon fillets with $1/2$ tablespoon vegetable oil and sprinkle with salt and pepper before grilling.*
- *Brush with Orange-Bourbon Glaze (page 122) during second half of grilling.*
- *Replace gremolata with Orange-Chive Gremolata (page 88).*

CRISP MUSHROOM-STUFFED SALMON

This is a super-easy entrée, yet delicious and impressive enough for guests. All of the following variations would also work well with halibut; especially the Leek & Sun-Dried Tomato option.

2 SLICES THICK-CUT BACON, CHOPPED
1½ CUPS CHOPPED CREMINI MUSHROOMS
1 MEDIUM SHALLOT, MINCED
3 OUNCES CREAM CHEESE, ROOM TEMPERATURE
1½ TABLESPOONS MINCED FRESH DILL
2 CUPS FRESH BREADCRUMBS
3 TABLESPOONS UNSALTED BUTTER, MELTED
¾ CUP GRATED PARMESAN CHEESE

¼ CUP MINCED ITALIAN PARSLEY
4 CENTER-CUT SALMON FILLETS, ABOUT 1½ INCHES THICK, 6–8 OUNCES EACH, SKINNED
SEA SALT AND FRESHLY GROUND PEPPER
1 TABLESPOON DIJON MUSTARD
1 TABLESPOON MAYONNAISE
DILL AND PARSLEY SPRIGS FOR GARNISH

Preheat oven to 450°.

Place a medium sauté pan over medium high heat. Add bacon and sauté for 4 minutes, or until browned. Remove bacon, with slotted spoon, to paper towels to drain. Add mushrooms and shallots to the same pan and sauté for 4 minutes, or until lightly browned. Place in a small bowl and mix in cream cheese, dill, and bacon. Cool for 5 minutes

Meanwhile, combine breadcrumbs, butter, Parmesan cheese, and minced parsley in another bowl.

Cut a vertical slit, lengthwise down the center of each salmon fillet, taking care not to cut through the bottom and leaving about ½ inch uncut at each end. Divide mushroom mixture evenly between salmon fillets, pressing into slits. Sprinkle fillets with salt and pepper.

In a small bowl or ramekin, mix together mustard and mayonnaise and spread over the tops of the salmon fillets.

Press breadcrumb mixture atop stuffed salmon fillets. Place fillets on a heavy, lightly oiled baking sheet. Bake salmon for 12–15 minutes or until crust is golden and salmon is cooked throughout. Remove salmon to platter or plates and garnish with dill and parsley sprigs if desired. Serves 4.

CLASSIC COMBOS

Spinach & Mascarpone Stuffed Salmon
- *Omit mushrooms.*
- *Add 4 ounces chopped fresh baby spinach to shallots after they have cooked for 1 minute and continue to cook until spinach has wilted, about 2 minutes.*
- *Replace cream cheese with 3 ounces mascarpone cheese.*
- *Replace dill with $\frac{1}{8}$ teaspoon nutmeg.*
- *Garnish with parsley sprigs.*

Blue Cheese & Walnut Stuffed Salmon
- *Replace mushrooms and minced shallot with $\frac{1}{2}$ cup thinly sliced shallots and $\frac{1}{3}$ cup chopped walnuts.*
- *Replace cream cheese with $\frac{1}{2}$ cup crumbled blue cheese.*
- *Replace dill with 2 teaspoons minced fresh rosemary.*
- *Garnish with rosemary and parsley sprigs.*

DARING PAIRINGS

Leek & Sun-Dried Tomato Stuffed Salmon
- *Replace mushrooms and minced shallot with $1\frac{1}{2}$ cups thinly sliced leeks and $\frac{1}{3}$ cup drained, chopped, oil-packed sun-dried tomatoes.*
- *Replace cream cheese with 3 ounces goat cheese.*
- *Replace dill with 2 tablespoons chopped fresh basil.*
- *Add 2 tablespoons toasted, chopped pine nuts to the breadcrumb mixture if desired.*
- *Garnish with basil and parsley sprigs.*

Cranberry & Pecan Stuffed Salmon
- *Replace mushrooms and minced shallot with $\frac{1}{2}$ cup thinly sliced shallot, $\frac{1}{3}$ cup chopped pecans and 2 teaspoons minced fresh thyme.*
- *Stir $\frac{1}{4}$ cup chopped dried cranberries into stuffing, along with cream cheese.*
- *Omit dill.*
- *Garnish with thyme and parsley sprigs.*

Sesame Seared Tuna with Oriental-Orange Mayo

Make sure you buy really fresh tuna and take care not to overcook it. Golden brown sesame seeds on the outside and bright pink, barely warm tuna on the inside is what we're going for here . . . fresh and delicious!

Tuna and Marinade

$^1/_4$ CUP SOY SAUCE

$^1/_4$ CUP DRY (OR MEDIUM DRY) SHERRY

1 TEASPOON RICE VINEGAR

$1^1/_2$ POUNDS 1-INCH THICK TUNA STEAKS (AHI/YELLOWFIN)

Oriental-Orange Mayo

$^1/_2$ TABLESPOON PEANUT OIL

$^1/_4$ CUP MINCED SCALLIONS (WHITE AND LIGHT GREEN PARTS ONLY)

1 TABLESPOON MINCED FRESH GINGER

1 TEASPOON MINCED FRESH GARLIC

4 TABLESPOONS JUICE PLUS 2 TEASPOONS GRATED ZEST FROM 1 ORANGE, DIVIDED

3 TABLESPOONS SOY SAUCE

2 TABLESPOONS RICE VINEGAR

1 TABLESPOON LIGHT BROWN SUGAR

2 WHOLE STAR ANISE

$^1/_2$ CUP MAYONNAISE

2 TABLESPOONS ASIAN SESAME OIL

SEA SALT AND FRESHLY GROUND PEPPER

$^2/_3$ CUP SESAME SEEDS

2 TABLESPOONS PEANUT OIL OR VEGETABLE OIL

2 TABLESPOONS MINCED FRESH CILANTRO PLUS SPRIGS FOR GARNISH (OPTIONAL)

In a small bowl whisk together $^1/_4$ cup soy sauce, sherry, and 1 teaspoon rice vinegar. Place tuna in a large, shallow dish or ziplock bag; add marinade, turning to coat tuna, and refrigerate for 30–60 minutes.

Meanwhile, make the mayo. In a small saucepan heat $^1/_2$ tablespoon peanut oil over medium-high heat. Add scallions, ginger, and garlic and sauté for 2 minutes. Add 2 tablespoons orange juice, soy sauce, rice vinegar, brown sugar, and star anise. Bring to a boil, stirring to dissolve the sugar. Reduce the heat and simmer for 10 minutes.

Cool slightly. Discard the star anise and remove the mixture to a blender or mini-processor. Add the remaining 2 tablespoons orange juice, orange zest, and mayonnaise and purée. Refrigerate until needed.

Remove the tuna steaks from the marinade, discarding marinade, and pat dry with paper towels. Rub tuna on both sides with sesame oil and sprinkle with salt and pepper. Coat both sides of steaks with sesame seeds, pressing to adhere.

In a large nonstick skillet heat 2 tablespoons peanut oil over medium-high heat. Add the tuna steaks and sear for 2 minutes or until seeds are golden brown. Turn over and cook for an additional 3 minutes for medium rare. Remove to a cutting board. If you prefer the tuna cooked to medium doneness, cover with foil and allow to rest for 5 minutes.

Slice tuna steaks into $1/4$-inch thick slices. Fan slices out on platter or plates and spoon mayo over the top. Sprinkle with minced cilantro and garnish with additional cilantro sprigs if desired. Pass remaining mayo separately. Serves 4.

CLASSIC COMBO

Sesame Seared Tuna Salad with Ginger-Lime Vinaigrette
- *Omit Oriental Orange Mayo.*
- *Serve sliced tuna atop a bed of mixed baby greens.*
- *Drizzle greens and tuna with Ginger-Lime Vinaigrette (page 116).*

DARING PAIRINGS

Mediterranean Seed Crusted Tuna with Romesco Mayo
- *Omit marinade.*
- *Replace Oriental Orange Mayo with Romesco Mayo (page 44).*
- *Replace Asian sesame oil with walnut oil.*
- *Replace sesame seeds with a mixture of 1 tablespoon crushed coriander seeds, 2 teaspoons crushed fennel seeds and 2 teaspoons crushed cumin seeds.*
- *Replace cilantro with Italian parsley.*

Sesame Seared Tuna with Wasabi Mayo & Ponzu Dipping Sauce
- *Omit Oriental Orange Mayo and cilantro.*
- *Place a dollop of Wasabi Mayo (page 42) atop each serving.*
- *Serve Ponzu Dipping Sauce (page 112) in individual bowls for dipping.*

Hawaiian Tuna Burgers with Maui Wowee Salsa

These burgers earned me the Grand Prize title and $20,000 at Sutter Home Winery's Build a Better Burger Cook-Off in 2000. Little did I know that a bumblebee found his way into the tuna mixture; and I ended up grilling him smack-dab in the middle of a burger! Luckily, none of the judges bit into that one!

Maui Wowee Salsa

2 cups chopped Maui onion (or other sweet onion)

1/2 cup minced scallions

1/4 cup drained and chopped pickled ginger (also called sushi ginger)

1/4 cup chopped cilantro

2 tablespoons Asian sesame oil

1 1/2 tablespoons soy sauce

1 tablespoon fresh lime juice

Tuna Burgers

2 pounds boneless, skinless Ahi (Yellowfin) tuna, finely chopped

1/2 cup panko

1 egg, lightly beaten

1/4 cup Dijon mustard

2 tablespoons minced fresh garlic

2 tablespoons honey

1 1/2 tablespoons Asian sesame oil

2 teaspoons coarse sea salt or kosher salt

1/2 teaspoon freshly ground pepper

1/4 teaspoon cayenne

vegetable oil

6 sesame seed buns, split

1/2 cup thick, bottled teriyaki sauce

Preheat the grill to medium-high heat.

Make the salsa. In a small bowl combine the salsa ingredients. Mix well and set aside to allow flavors to blend.

In a large bowl combine the tuna, panko, egg, mustard, garlic, honey, sesame oil, salt, pepper, and cayenne and mix well. Shape into 6 1/2-inch-thick patties. Brush the grill with vegetable oil and cook tuna burgers over direct heat until barely cooked throughout, about 4 minutes per side.

During the last 2 minutes of grilling, place the buns, cut sides down, on outside of grill to toast lightly. Brush both halves of buns with teriyaki sauce. Place a tuna burger on the bottom half of each bun, then top with salsa and the top of the bun. Serves 6.

Notes

Burgers can also be broiled or cooked atop the stove in a ridged grill pan or on a griddle.

CLASSIC COMBOS

Teriyaki Tuna Burgers with Cucumber-Pineapple Salsa
- *Replace salsa with Cucumber-Pineapple Salsa (page 66).*
- *Chop the cucumber and pineapple into smaller pieces.*
- *Reduce Dijon mustard to 2 tablespoons.*
- *Omit sesame oil and honey.*
- *Add ¼ cup teriyaki sauce to burger mixture.*

Honey-Mustard Tuna Burgers
- *Replace salsa with fresh watercress or baby arugula leaves.*
- *Replace half of the Dijon mustard with coarse grained mustard.*
- *Increase the honey to 3 tablespoons.*
- *Omit sesame oil.*
- *Add 2 teaspoons ground fennel seed to burgers.*
- *Replace teriyaki sauce with Lemon-Tarragon Aioli (page 46).*
- *Replace sesame buns with onion buns.*

DARING PAIRINGS

Sushi Burgers with Wasabi Mayo
- *Replace salsa with 1 sliced avocado.*
- *Increase panko to 1 cup.*
- *Reduce Dijon mustard to 2 tablespoons.*
- *Add 1½ tablespoons soy sauce, ¼ cup minced scallions and ¼ cup chopped pickled (sushi) ginger to burgers.*
- *Reduce coarse salt to 1 teaspoon.*
- *Replace teriyaki sauce with Wasabi Mayo (page 42).*

Sicilian Tuna Burgers with Caponata
- *Replace salsa with Roasted Eggplant-Pepper Caponata (page 81).*
- *Omit sesame oil.*
- *Add 2 teaspoons grated lemon zest, 1 teaspoon ground coriander, ½ teaspoon ground fennel, and ¼ cup chopped Italian parsley to burgers.*
- *Omit teriyaki sauce.*
- *Replace sesame buns with focaccia bread or onion buns.*

MOJO GRILLED SEA BASS WITH FLORIBBEAN SALSA

The fresh citrus and tropical fruit flavors here are the perfect counterpoint to rich, buttery sea bass. Don't leave the sea bass in the marinade for longer than an hour or the lime juice will start to "cook" it!

MOJO MARINADE

$3/4$ CUP FRESH ORANGE JUICE

$1/2$ CUP CHOPPED SWEET ONION

$1/4$ CUP FRESH LIME JUICE

$1/4$ CUP GRAND MARNIER OR OTHER ORANGE LIQUEUR

$1/4$ CUP EXTRA VIRGIN OLIVE OIL

$1/4$ CUP SOY SAUCE

2 TABLESPOONS CHOPPED FRESH GARLIC

2 TABLESPOONS CHOPPED FRESH OREGANO OR 2 TEASPOONS DRIED

$1^1/_2$ TEASPOONS GROUND CUMIN

$1^1/_2$ TEASPOON FRESHLY GROUND PEPPER

1 TEASPONS GRATED LIME ZEST

6 SEA BASS FILLETS, ABOUT 7 TO 8 OUNCES EACH, SKINNED

FLORIBBEAN SALSA

2 TABLESPOONS OLIVE OIL

2 1-INCH THICK ROUND SLICES OF FRESH PINEAPPLE

1 RED BELL PEPPER, QUARTERED AND SEEDED

2 TO 3 JALAPEÑO PEPPERS, HALVED AND SEEDED

1 BUNCH SCALLIONS, TRIMMED

1 CUP DICED FRESH PAPAYA

1 ORANGE, ZEST GRATED, SEGMENTS REMOVED AND CHOPPED

$1/4$ CUP MINCED FRESH CILANTRO

2 TABLESPOONS FRESH LIME JUICE, PLUS MORE TO TASTE

SEA SALT AND FRESHLY GROUND PEPPER

HABANERO HOT SAUCE TO TASTE

LIME WEDGES FOR GARNISH

In a blender combine all marinade ingredients and purée. Remove 2 tablespoons marinade to a small bowl or ramekin and set aside. Pour the remaining marinade into a large, heavy duty ziplock bag; add the sea bass and place in the refrigerator for 1 hour. Turn the bag occasionally.

Meanwhile, preheat the grill to medium-high heat.

Whisk the olive oil into the reserved marinade. Brush over the pineapple slices, jalapeños, and scallions.

Grill the pineapple slices, jalapeños, and scallions until lightly charred and slightly softened; turning and moving around the grill as needed. This should take about 4 to 8 minutes. Remove the items to a cutting board as they are done.

Cut the rind off the pineapple, remove the core, and chop the flesh. Place in a large bowl. Chop the jalapeños and scallions and add to the pineapple.

Add the papaya, orange zest, chopped orange, cilantro, and lime juice. Mix thoroughly and season to taste with salt, pepper, and hot sauce.

Remove the fish from the marinade and discard marinade. Oil grill grate or fish basket and grill fish over direct heat until just cooked though, about 4 to 6 minutes per side.

Place the fish on a platter or plates. Top with salsa and serve with lime wedges. Serves 6.

NOTES

Sea bass can also be broiled.

CLASSIC COMBO

Teriyaki Grilled Sea Bass with Coconut-Corn Salsa
- *Replace marinade with Teriyaki Marinade (page 16) for up to 2 hours.*
- *Replace salsa with Coconut-Corn Salsa (page 64).*
- *Don't forget to set aside 2 tablespoons of the marinade to make the salsa.*
- *Omit lime wedges. Garnish with cilantro sprigs.*

DARING PAIRINGS

Miso Grilled Sea Bass with Edamame Salsa
- *Replace marinade with Miso-Mustard Marinade (page 18) for up to 2 hours.*
- *Replace salsa with Edamame Salsa (page 65).*
- *Omit lime wedges. Garnish with cilantro sprigs.*

Masala-Spiced Sea Bass with Pineapple-Coconut Raita
- *Replace marinade with a mixture of 2$\frac{1}{2}$ tablespoons Curry-Masala Rub (page 37) and 2 tablespoons olive oil rubbed over fillets 15–30 minutes before grilling.*
- *Replace salsa with a double recipe of Pineapple-Coconut Raita (page 76).*
- *Omit lime wedges. Garnish with cilantro and mint sprigs.*
- *This variation can also be successfully pan-seared.*

Margarita Swordfish with Tomato-Mango Salsa

You'll want to whip up a big pitcher of margaritas to serve with this lively dish! You'll have more salsa than you need for the fish. Serve some before or during dinner with tortilla chips.

MARGARITA MARINADE

1/2 CUP MINCED SWEET ONION

1/2 CUP FRESH LIME JUICE

6 TABLESPOONS TEQUILA

1/4 CUP FROZEN ORANGE JUICE CONCENTRATE, THAWED

2 TABLESPOONS MINCED FRESH GARLIC

2 TABLESPOONS OLIVE OIL

2 TEASPOONS DRIED OREGANO (MEXICAN PREFERRED)

2 TEASPOONS CHIPOTLE CHILE POWDER

2 TEASPOONS GROUND CUMIN

6 1-INCH THICK SWORDFISH STEAKS, ABOUT 7 OUNCES EACH

TOMATO-MANGO SALSA

3 CUPS SEEDED, CHOPPED RIPE TOMATOES

2 RIPE MANGOES, FLESH CHOPPED

1 CUP MINCED RED ONION OR SWEET ONION

1 CUP MINCED MIXED CHILE PEPPERS (RED AND GREEN JALAPEÑOS, SERRANOS, ANAHEIMS, ETC.)

3/4 CUP MINCED FRESH CILANTRO

JUICE AND GRATED ZEST FROM 1 LIME

2 TABLESPOONS EXTRA VIRGIN OLIVE OIL

1 TABLESPOON MINCED FRESH GARLIC

1 TABLESPOON SHERRY VINEGAR OR RASPBERRY VINEGAR (OPTIONAL)

1 1/2 TEASPOON GROUND CUMIN

1 TEASPOON DRIED OREGANO (MEXICAN PREFERRED)

HABANERO HOT SAUCE TO TASTE (OPTIONAL)

SEA SALT AND FRESHLY GROUND PEPPER

OLIVE OIL

CILANTRO SPRIGS FOR GARNISH

In a blender combine the marinade ingredients and purée. Remove to a large ziplock bag, add the swordfish steaks, and marinate, refrigerated, for 1 to 1 1/2 hours.

Meanwhile, prepare the salsa by combining the salsa ingredients in a large bowl. Season to taste with salt and pepper. Leave at room temperature for 30 minutes or refrigerate for up to 2 hours.

Preheat the grill to medium-high heat. Remove the swordfish from the marinade and season with salt and pepper. Oil the grill and grill the fish, directly over the heat, until it is no longer opaque in the center, about 4 to 5 minutes per side.

Place the swordfish steaks on plates or a platter. Spoon salsa generously over the fish, using a slotted spoon. Garnish with cilantro sprigs if desired. Serves 6.

Notes

Swordfish can also be broiled or cooked atop the stove in a ridged grill pan.

Classic Combo

Cypress Swordfish with Greek Salsa
- *Replace marinade with Cypress-Style Marinade (page 23).*
- *Replace salsa with Greek Salsa (page 72).*
- *Garnish with parsley or mint sprigs.*

Daring Pairings

Mojo Swordfish with Savory Caribbean Salsa
- *Replace marinade with Mojo Marinade (page 20).*
- *Replace salsa with a double recipe of Savory Caribbean Salsa (page 71).*

Sicilian Swordfish with Caponata
- *Replace marinade with Rosemary-Lemon Marinade (page 22).*
- *Replace salsa with Roasted Eggplant-Pepper Caponata (page 81).*
- *Garnish with parsley sprigs.*

Swordfish Souvlaki with Fennel & Sun-Dried Tomato Tzatziki

Souvlaki is a Greek shish kabob, usually made with pork. Swordfish is meaty enough to hang tight to the skewers and tastes great with a variety marinades, sauces, and relishes. Halibut and marlin would also work well in these recipes.

PEPPERED GREEK MARINADE

- $^2/_3$ CUP EXTRA VIRGIN OLIVE OIL
  JUICE AND GRATED ZEST OF 1 LEMON
- $^1/_4$ CUP DRY WHITE WINE
- 1 TABLESPOON MINCED FRESH GARLIC
- 2 TEASPOONS DRIED OREGANO (PREFERABLY GREEK OR TURKISH)
- 1 BAY LEAF
- 1 TEASPOON COARSE SEA SALT OR KOSHER SALT
- $^1/_2$ TEASPOON FRESHLY GROUND PEPPER
- 1 TEASPOON ALEPPO PEPPER FLAKES (OPTIONAL)

$1^1/_2$ POUNDS SWORDFISH, CUT INTO $1^1/_2$-INCH CHUNKS

FENNEL & SUN-DRIED TOMATO TZATZIKI

- 1 CUP PLAIN YOGURT (NOT FAT FREE)
- 1 CUP SEEDED, DICED CUCUMBER
- $^1/_2$ CUP FINELY MINCED FENNEL BULB
- $^1/_4$ CUP MINCED SUN-DRIED TOMATO (OIL-PACKED, DRAINED)
- 2 TABLESPOONS FINELY MINCED RED ONION
- 2 TABLESPOONS CHOPPED FENNEL FRONDS
- 2 TEASPOONS FRESH LEMON JUICE
- 1 TEASPOON GRATED LEMON ZEST
- 1 GARLIC CLOVE, MINCED

  SEA SALT AND FRESHLY GROUND PEPPER
- 1 LARGE GREEN OR RED BELL PEPPER, CUT INTO 1-INCH PIECES
- 1 LARGE RED ONION, CUT INTO 1-INCH PIECES
- 2 TABLESPOONS OLIVE OIL

In a medium bowl whisk together the marinade ingredients. Place the marinade and swordfish in a large ziplock plastic bag and refrigerate for $1^1/_2$ to 2 hours, turning the bag occasionally.

Meanwhile, in a medium bowl combine the tzatziki ingredients. Season to taste with salt and pepper. If not using immediately, cover and refrigerate.

Preheat the grill to medium-high heat. Remove the swordfish from the marinade and discard the marinade. Toss the bell pepper and onion pieces with olive oil. Thread the swordfish, pepper, and onion pieces alternately onto 8 long metal skewers. Sprinkle lightly with salt and pepper.

Grill the souvlaki over direct heat until just cooked through, about 6 to 8 minutes, turning frequently. Place the skewers on a platter or plates and serve tzatziki alongside. Serves 4.

MAKE IT YOUR OWN

NOTES

Skewers can also be broiled.

CLASSIC COMBO

Provençal Fish Brochettes on Roasted Ratatouille Relish
- *Replace marinade with Provençal Herb Marinade (page 31).*
- *Replace half of swordfish with halibut.*
- *Replace tzatziki with Roasted Ratatouille Relish (page 82).*
- *Omit bell pepper and onion.*
- *Serve brochettes atop a bed of the relish.*

DARING PAIRING

Citrus Swordfish Skewers with Chimichurri
- *Replace marinade with Mojo Marinade (page 20).*
- *Replace tzatziki with Chimichurri Sauce (page 64), spooned over the skewers.*
- *Omit bell pepper.*

POULTRY

With these recipes you'll discover that poultry definitely does not have to be boring! Chicken, turkey, and game hens all work well with a wide variety of flavors, as you'll see here.

Poblano Stuffed Chicken with Pancetta-Corn Salsa

Pan seared chicken breasts have a tendency to become dry during cooking. The cheesy filings here keep them nice and moist, as does covering the pan during cooking.

1 LARGE POBLANO PEPPER	1 TABLESPOON FRESH LIME JUICE
	SEA SALT AND FRESHLY CRACKED PEPPER TO TASTE
PANCETTA-CORN SALSA	**STUFFED CHICKEN**
2 TABLESPOONS OLIVE OIL	$^1/_2$ CUP CRUMBLED FETA CHEESE
2 CUPS FRESH CORN KERNELS (ABOUT 2 LARGE EARS)	1 TEASPOON ROASTED GARLIC (PAGE 8 OR STORE BOUGHT)
$^3/_4$ CUP DICED RED BELL PEPPER	SALT AND PEPPER TO TASTE
2 OUNCES PANCETTA, CHOPPED	4 LARGE BONELESS, SKINLESS CHICKEN BREASTS
1 BUNCH SCALLIONS, MINCED	$1^1/_2$ TABLESPOONS CRUSHED CORIANDER SEEDS
1 TO 2 JALAPEÑO PEPPERS, SEEDED AND MINCED	$1^1/_2$ TABLESPOONS CRUSHED CUMIN SEEDS
1 TEASPOON MINCED FRESH GARLIC	2 TABLESPOONS OLIVE OIL
$^1/_2$ TEASPOON DRIED OREGANO (MEXICAN PREFERRED)	CILANTRO SPRIGS FOR GARNISH
2 TABLESPOONS MINCED FRESH CILANTRO	

Char the poblano pepper directly over a gas flame or under the broiler until blackened all over. Enclose in a small paper bag for 10 minutes, then peel, seed, and chop.

Meanwhile, make the salsa. In a large skillet heat the olive oil over medium-high heat. Add the corn, red pepper, and pancetta and sauté for 10 minutes. Add the scallions, jalapeños, garlic, and oregano and sauté for 2 minutes. Remove from the heat. Stir in the cilantro and lime juice. Season to taste with salt and pepper. Set aside.

In a small bowl mix together the chopped poblano pepper, crumbled feta cheese, and roasted garlic. Season stuffing with salt and pepper.

Cut a slit thru the side of each chicken breast, forming an internal pocket, taking care not to cut through the bottom or sides. Divide the pepper mixture between breasts, stuffing into pockets. Press opening closed. Sprinkle stuffed breasts with salt and pepper.

In a shallow bowl combine the coriander and cumin seeds. Coat the chicken breasts evenly with the seeds, pressing to adhere.

In a large nonstick skillet heat 2 tablespoons olive oil over medium-high heat. Add the chicken, top side down, and cook until nicely browned, about 6 minutes. Flip over, cover pan, reduce the heat to medium, and continue to cook until chicken is cooked through, about 8–10 more minutes. Internal temperature should be 160°.

Remove breasts to cutting board and let rest 5 minutes. Slightly re-warm salsa and spoon onto platter or plates. Slice breasts in half, on the diagonal, and arrange atop salsa. Garnish with cilantro sprigs if desired. Serves 4.

Notes

If you can't find a poblano pepper, roasted red peppers are also delicious.

Classic Combo

Coriander-Feta Chicken on Greek Salsa
- *Replace poblano pepper in stuffing with 1/4 cup minced, oil-packed sun-dried tomatoes, drained.*
- *Replace salsa with Greek Salsa (page 72)*
- *Replace cumin seeds with an additional 1½ tablespoons crushed coriander seeds.*
- *Garnish with parsley or mint sprigs.*

Daring Pairing

Pesto Chicken on Ratatouille Relish
- *Replace poblano pepper in stuffing with 2 tablespoons minced, oil-packed sun-dried tomatoes and 2 tablespoons Basil-Mint Pesto (page 104 or store-bought basil pesto)*
- *Replace salsa with Roasted Ratatouille Relish (page 82)*
- *Replace cumin seeds with 1½ tablespoons crushed fennel seeds.*
- *Garnish with parsley, basil or oregano sprigs.*

Bruschetta Chicken with Two-Tomato Vinaigrette

The crisp breading on the chicken, along with the fresh tomato and basil flavors in this dish, will remind you of its namesake, bruschetta. All of the variations here would be great for entertaining, as the chicken can be stuffed and the topping prepared, a few hours in advance.

Two-Tomato Vinaigrette

- 1/4 CUP FRUITY EXTRA VIRGIN OLIVE OIL
- 1/4 CUP CHOPPED SHALLOTS
- 1 TABLESPOON MINCED FRESH GARLIC
- 1 1/2 CUPS HALVED CHERRY TOMATOES
- 1 1/2 CUPS HALVED YELLOW PEAR TOMATOES
- 2 TABLESPOONS WHITE BALSAMIC VINEGAR
- 1 TABLESPOON SUGAR
- SEA SALT AND FRESHLY GROUND PEPPER
- 2 TABLESPOONS CHOPPED FRESH BASIL

Bruschetta Chicken

- 4 LONG, THIN SLICES PROSCIUTTO
- 1/2 CUP FRESHLY GRATED FONTINA CHEESE
- 16 LARGE BASIL LEAVES
- 2 CUPS FRESH BREADCRUMBS
- 1/2 CUP FRESHLY GRATED PARMESAN CHEESE
- 3 TABLESPOONS MINCED FRESH ITALIAN PARSLEY
- 3 TABLESPOONS UNSALTED BUTTER, MELTED
- 4 LARGE BONELESS, SKINLESS CHICKEN BREASTS
- SEA SALT AND FRESHLY GROUND PEPPER
- 1 TABLESPOON DIJON MUSTARD
- ITALIAN PARSLEY SPRIGS FOR GARNISH

Preheat the oven to 425°. Spray a large, heavy baking sheet with nonstick cooking spray.

Make the vinaigrette. In a medium sauté pan heat the olive oil over medium heat. Add the shallots and garlic and sauté for 3 minutes. Add the tomatoes and sauté for 3 minutes. Add the vinegar and sugar and simmer for 2 minutes. Remove from the heat and season to taste with salt and pepper. Stir in basil and set aside.

Lay prosciutto slices on work surface. Scatter the fontina evenly over the top of each slice. Lay basil leaves over cheese. Starting at one end, roll up the prosciutto slices, jellyroll style, to enclose the cheese and basil.

In a small bowl combine the breadcrumbs with the Parmesan, parsley, and melted butter.

Cut a slit thru the side of each chicken breast, forming an internal pocket about the length of the prosciutto roll. Stuff each pocket with a roll and press opening together to close. Sprinkle chicken with salt and pepper. Spread mustard over tops of breasts. Press the breadcrumb mixture over tops of breasts. Place chicken on the prepared baking sheet and bake for 15–20 minutes, or until the chicken is cooked through (160°) and the breadcrumb coating is golden brown and crisp. Remove from the oven and let chicken rest for 5 minutes.

Slice chicken breasts into ³/₄-inch thick slices and fan out on plates or platter. Spoon vinaigrette over slices. Garnish with parsley sprigs if desired. Serves 4.

CLASSIC COMBO

Bruschetta Chicken Pasta
- *Omit vinaigrette.*
- *Fan chicken slices atop a bed of spaghetti covered in Red Wine Marinara (page 100).*

DARING PAIRINGS

Bourbon Street Chicken with Sweet Corn Remoulade
- *Replace vinaigrette with Sweet Corn Remoulade (page 50).*
- *Replace prosciutto with thinly sliced deli ham.*
- *Omit basil and fontina cheese.*
- *For filling, sauté ¹/₂ cup minced onion and ¹/₂ cup minced green bell pepper in 1 tablespoon olive oil until softened. Mix in 2 teaspoons Cajun-Creole Spice Rub (page 34 or store-bought.) Cool slightly, spread mixture over ham and proceed with recipe.*
- *Fan chicken slices atop a bed of remoulade.*
- *If you are using a purchased Cajun spice blend, check the salt level and adjust accordingly.*

Barcelona Chicken with Sautéed Mushroom Vinaigrette
- *Replace vinaigrette with Sautéed Mushroom Vinaigrette (page 114).*
- *Replace prosciutto with Serrano ham (optional.)*
- *Replace basil with baby spinach leaves.*
- *Replace fontina cheese with ¹/₂ cup grated Manchego cheese tossed with ¹/₂ cup chopped roasted red pepper (page 9 or store-bought).*

Cajun Chicken & Sweet Potatoes

I love using a whole chicken . . . everyone gets their favorite parts! If you don't want to use the wings, stash them in the freezer until the next time you make stock. Serve a scoop of rice or couscous alongside, to soak up the flavorful sauce.

2	TABLESPOONS OLIVE OIL	2	TABLESPOONS TOMATO PASTE
2	3-OUNCE ANDOUILLE SAUSAGES, SLICED $1/4$-INCH THICK	1	TABLESPOON CAJUN-CREOLE SPICE RUB (PAGE 34 OR STORE-BOUGHT)
1	WHOLE, CUT-UP, CHICKEN, TRIMMED OF ANY EXCESS FAT	1	TEASPOON DRIED OREGANO
	SEA SALT AND FRESHLY GROUND PEPPER	4	CUPS SWEET POTATOES, PEELED AND CUT INTO $3/4$-INCH CHUNKS (ABOUT 2 LARGE)
2	CUPS LOW SODIUM CHICKEN BROTH OR HOMEMADE STOCK	$1/4$	CUP MINCED ITALIAN PARSLEY, DIVIDED
2	CUPS HALVED AND THINLY SLICED ONION	2	TABLESPOONS WORCESTERSHIRE SAUCE
$1^1/2$	CUPS THIN SLICES RED BELL PEPPER	1	BAY LEAF
1	CUP THIN SLICES GREEN BELL PEPPER	1	TABLESPOON UNSALTED BUTTER, SOFTENED
1	TABLESPOON MINCED FRESH GARLIC	1	TABLESPOON FLOUR
1	TABLESPOON MINCED FRESH THYME LEAVES		PARSLEY AND THYME SPRIGS FOR GARNISH

In a Dutch oven or other large heavy pot heat 1 tablespoon oil over medium-high heat. Add sausage and sauté for 4 minutes or until browned. Remove and set aside. Sprinkle chicken pieces generously with salt and pepper. Add half of the chicken to the pot and brown evenly, about 7–8 minutes. Remove from pot and set aside. Add remaining 1 tablespoon oil to pot and repeat with remaining chicken pieces. Remove from pot and set aside.

Add $1/2$ cup chicken broth to pot and scrape to loosen browned bits. Cook until almost evaporated. Add onion and bell pepper slices to pot and sauté until softened and beginning to brown, about 8 minutes. Add garlic, thyme, tomato paste, Cajun seasoning, and oregano and cook, stirring constantly, for 1 minute. Stir in the reserved sausage, remaining broth, sweet potatoes, 2 tablespoons parsley, Worcestershire, and bay leaf and bring to a boil. Place the chicken pieces atop the other ingredients, cover, reduce heat, and simmer for 35 minutes or until chicken is cooked through and potatoes are tender.

Remove chicken pieces to serving dish. Discard bay leaf. In a small bowl mash together butter and flour and whisk into sweet potato mixture. Bring to a boil and boil for 2 minutes, stirring. Spoon mixture over and around chicken pieces and sprinkle with remaining parsley. Garnish with parsley and thyme sprigs if desired.

Notes

If you are using a purchased Cajun-Creole spice blend, check the salt level and package directions, and adjust accordingly.

Classic Combo

Moroccan Chicken & Squash Tagine
- *Omit sausage and bell peppers.*
- *Add 1 tablespoon minced fresh ginger, 1 seeded and minced jalapeño, 1 teaspoon ground cinnamon, 1/2 teaspoon ground cumin, and 1/2 teaspoon ground coriander with the garlic and thyme.*
- *Omit tomato paste, Cajun seasoning and oregano.*
- *Replace sweet potatoes with butternut squash plus 1/3 cup chopped dried apricots.*
- *Omit Worcestershire and bay leaf.*
- *Sprinkle 1/4 cup sliced, toasted almonds over finished dish, along with reserved parsley.*

Daring Pairing

Spanish Chicken & Chick Peas
- *Replace andouille sausage with chorizo sausage.*
- *Omit green bell pepper.*
- *Replace 1/2 cup broth with medium dry sherry; use to deglaze pan.*
- *Add 2 teaspoons Spanish smoked paprika (pimentón) and 1 teaspoon ground cumin with the garlic, thyme and tomato paste.*
- *Omit Cajun seasoning and oregano.*
- *Replace sweet potatoes with 1 15-ounce can diced tomatoes, drained and 1 15-ounce can chick peas, drained and rinsed.*
- *Replace Worcestershire with sherry vinegar.*
- *Sprinkle 1/4 cup sliced, toasted almonds over finished dish, along with reserved parsley.*

BIFF'S BEER CAN CHICKEN

My best friend Jeff (AKA Biff Malibu) created this tasty chicken dish for one of his many backyard barbecues in Southern California. For those of us with snow covering our grills for months on end, the chicken is equally delicious roasted in a 325° oven.

MARINADE

$1/2$ CUP EXTRA VIRGIN OLIVE OIL

　JUICE AND GRATED ZEST OF 1 LEMON
　(MEYER LEMON PREFERRED)

　JUICE AND GRATED ZEST OF 1 LIME

$1/4$ CUP CHOPPED FRESH GARLIC

$1/4$ CUP CHOPPED FRESH ROSEMARY

$1^1/2$ TABLESPOONS CAJUN-CREOLE SPICE RUB
　(PAGE 34 OR STORE-BOUGHT)

1　$3^1/2$ TO 4 POUND CHICKEN

　SEA SALT AND FRESHLY GROUND PEPPER

1　CAN BEER

$1/2$　TABLESPOON CAJUN-CREOLE SPICE RUB

　MEYER LEMON WEDGES AND ROSEMARY
　SPRIGS FOR GARNISH

Make the marinade. Combine the marinade ingredients in a large, heavy-duty ziplock bag. Gently loosen the skin from the chicken by running your hands underneath it, being careful not to tear the skin. Add chicken to the bag, pushing some of the marinade under the skin and rubbing some inside the cavity of the chicken. Marinate, refrigerated, for at least 4 hours and up to 12, turning the bag occasionally.

Preheat the grill to medium heat (325°). Remove the chicken from the marinade and season, inside and out, with salt and pepper. Open the beer can and take a few sips. With a church-key style opener, punch a few more holes in the top of the can. Slowly spoon $1/2$ tablespoon Cajun-Creole Spice Rub into the can. Holding the chicken upright, with the opening of the body cavity down, insert the beer can into the cavity. Place the chicken, upright, in a disposable foil roasting pan, adjusting to balance on the beer can.

Place the pan on the grill, cover, and cook until the chicken is "fall-off-the-bone tender," about $1^1/2$–2 hours. If you are using a charcoal grill, you will need to add about 20 coals to the grill after the first hour. The temperature in the thickest part of the thigh should be at least 170°.

Using tongs and a large spatula for support, lift the bird onto a serving platter. Garnish the platter with lemon wedges and rosemary sprigs if desired. Let chicken rest 10–20 minutes before carving. Serves 4.

NOTES

- If you are using a purchased Cajun-Creole spice blend, be sure to check the salt level and package directions, and adjust accordingly.
- If you are preparing the chicken in the oven, you can use a regular roasting pan, rather than a disposable one. Don't use a nonstick pan or the beer can may scratch the surface.

CLASSIC COMBOS

Southwest Beer Can Chicken

- *Omit lemon juice and zest.*
- *Replace rosemary with oregano.*
- *Replace spice rub with Southwest Spice Rub (page 34 or store-bought).*
- *Garnish with lime wedges and oregano sprigs.*
- *If using a purchased Southwest spice blend, check the salt level and package directions and adjust accordingly.*

Jerk Beer Can Chicken

- *Replace marinade with Jamaican Jerk Marinade (page 32).*
- *Replace spice rub in beer can with whole allspice.*
- *Garnish with thyme sprigs.*

DARING PAIRINGS

Tuscan-Herb Beer Can Chicken

- *Replace marinade with a double recipe of Tuscan Herb Paste (page 30).*
- *Replace spice rub in beer can with lightly crushed fennel seeds.*
- *Garnish with herb sprigs leftover from making herb paste.*

Thai Lemongrass Beer Can Chicken

- *Replace marinade with Thai Lemongrass Marinade (page 14).*
- *Replace spice rub in beer can with some of the unused lemongrass stalk.*
- *Garnish with cilantro sprigs.*

CHICKEN & WILD MUSHROOM RISOTTO WITH ROASTED GARLIC

A rich and creamy bowl of risotto makes a satisfying dinner on a chilly winter evening. Just add a crisp green salad and you're good to go!

WILD MUSHROOM RISOTTO WITH ROASTED GARLIC

1/2 OUNCE DRIED PORCINI MUSHROOMS

2 TABLESPOONS OLIVE OIL, DIVIDED

4 OUNCES SHIITAKE MUSHROOM CAPS, QUARTERED

8 OUNCES BUTTON MUSHROOMS, THICKLY SLICED

2/3 CUP CHOPPED SHALLOTS

1 CUP ARBORIO RICE

1 1/2 TABLESPOONS MINCED FRESH ROSEMARY

1/2 CUP DRY WHITE WINE

3 CUPS LOW SALT CHICKEN BROTH, WARMED IN A SMALL SAUCEPAN

2 TABLESPOONS ROASTED GARLIC (PAGE 8 OR STORE-BOUGHT)

1 CUP FRESHLY GRATED PARMESAN CHEESE

2 TABLESPOONS CHOPPED FRESH ITALIAN PARSLEY

SAUTEED CHICKEN

2 TABLESPOONS OLIVE OIL

1 TO 1 1/2 POUNDS BONELESS, SKINLESS CHICKEN BREASTS, CUT INTO BITE-SIZED PIECES

SEA SALT AND FRESHLY GROUND PEPPER

Soak porcinis in 1 cup boiling water for 20 minutes. Remove and chop mushrooms. Reserve soaking liquid.

In a large skillet heat 1 tablespoon olive oil over medium-high heat. Add shiitake and button mushrooms and sauté for 7 minutes or until all of the liquid they release has evaporated and they are beginning to brown. Add porcinis and about 1/2 cup of the soaking liquid, leaving any grit behind. Cook until all liquid has evaporated. Remove mushrooms to a bowl. Reserve the skillet for cooking chicken.

In a medium saucepan heat 1 tablespoon olive oil over medium heat. Add shallots and sauté for 3 minutes. Add rice and rosemary and stir for 1 minute. Add wine and cook, stirring, until liquid has evaporated. Add broth, about 1/2 cup at a time, stirring frequently and waiting until each addition has been absorbed before adding the next. Continue until rice is tender and creamy, about 20–25 minutes.

Meanwhile, in the reserved skillet heat 2 tablespoons olive oil over medium-high heat. Sprinkle the chicken with salt and pepper, add to the skillet, and sauté until cooked throughout, about 5 minutes.

During the last few minutes of cooking the risotto, add the reserved mushrooms, chicken, and roasted garlic. Remove risotto to large serving bowl. Stir in the Parmesan cheese, sprinkle with parsley, and serve. Serves 4.

Classic Combo

Chicken-Apple Sausage & Butternut Risotto
- *Omit all mushrooms.*
- *Add 2 teaspoons chopped fresh garlic with shallots and omit roasted garlic.*
- *Replace chicken with 1 pound fully cooked chicken & apple sausages, sliced 1/4 inch thick and sautéed in olive oil until lightly browned.*
- *Add 3 cups cooked butternut squash to risotto with sausage. (Cut squash into 1-inch pieces; toss with 1 tablespoon olive oil; spread out on a baking sheet and roast in a 400° oven for 25–30 minutes or until browned and tender.)*

Daring Pairings

Lemony Chicken Risotto with Fennel & Sugar Snaps
- *Omit all mushrooms.*
- *Add 1 chopped fennel bulb with shallots and increase sautéeing time to 5 minutes.*
- *Omit rosemary.*
- *Add 1/2 teaspoon pure vanilla extract to chicken broth.*
- *Add 8 ounces steamed sugar snap peas, 2 tablespoons fresh lemon juice and 1 teaspoon grated lemon zest to risotto with chicken.*
- *Omit roasted garlic.*
- *Replace parsley with fennel fronds.*

Herbed Turkey, Mushroom & Cranberry Risotto
- *Add 2 teaspoons minced fresh garlic with shallots and omit roasted garlic.*
- *Add 1 1/2 tablespoons chopped fresh sage with rosemary.*
- *Add 2/3 cup dried cranberries, about halfway through cooking risotto.*
- *Replace chicken with turkey tenderloin.*
- *Add 1/4 cup chopped, toasted pecans with Parmesan cheese.*

CRANBERRY & HERB GAME HENS ON WILD RICE BUTTERNUT PILAF

Game hens make for an elegant dinner party entrée yet are economical and simple to prepare. Halving the hens is a snap! Just cut out the back bone with a pair of kitchen shears and then cut through the center of the breastbone with a sharp knife. Feel free to halve the hens and rub the herb butter under the skin up to 8 hours in advance. Cover and refrigerate them until you're ready to cook. The pilaf can also be made a couple of hours in advance and left at room temperature. Reheat and add the pecans and parsley just before serving.

2 TABLESPOONS BRANDY OR DRY WHITE WINE

2 TABLESPOONS DRIED CRANBERRIES

WILD RICE BUTTERNUT PILAF

2 TABLESPOONS OLIVE OIL

1 CUP CHOPPED SWEET ONION

4 GARLIC CLOVES, MINCED

3 CUPS THINLY SLICED CREMINI MUSHROOMS (6 OUNCES)

$3/4$ CUP WILD RICE

$1/2$ CUP DRY WHITE WINE

1 TABLESPOON EACH MINCED FRESH SAGE, ROSEMARY AND THYME

2 CUPS LOW SODIUM CHICKEN BROTH OR HOMEMADE STOCK

3 CUPS PEELED AND SEEDED BUTTERNUT SQUASH, CUT INTO 1-INCH PIECES

$1/2$ CUP DRIED CRANBERRIES

SEA SALT AND FRESHLY GROUND PEPPER

$1/4$ CUP CHOPPED PECANS

3 TABLESPOONS CHOPPED FRESH ITALIAN PARSLEY

CRANBERRY & HERB GAME HENS

$1/2$ TABLESPOON EACH MINCED FRESH SAGE, ROSEMARY AND THYME

4 TABLESPOONS UNSALTED BUTTER, SOFTENED

SEA SALT AND FRESHLY GROUND PEPPER

2 LARGE CORNISH GAME HENS, ABOUT 24 OUNCES EACH, HALVED

1 TABLESPOON OLIVE OIL

PARSLEY, SAGE, ROSEMARY, AND THYME SPRIGS FOR GARNISH

Preheat oven to 400°. Before beginning the pilaf, place brandy in a ramekin or small bowl and heat to boiling in the microwave. Add 2 tablespoons cranberries, cover with plastic wrap, and set aside.

Make pilaf. In a large saucepan heat 2 tablespoons oil over medium-high heat. Add the onion, garlic, and mushrooms and sauté until softened, about 8–10 minutes. Meanwhile, in a large, nonstick, ovenproof skillet toast the wild rice over medium heat for 4 minutes, stirring frequently. Remove the rice and reserve the skillet for cooking the hens.

Add wine to the onion mixture and simmer until evaporated, about 3 minutes. Add rice, minced fresh herbs, and chicken broth. Bring to a boil; reduce heat, cover with a tight fitting lid, and simmer for 30 minutes. Stir in squash, return to a boil, cover, and simmer for 10 minutes. Stir in ½ cup cranberries, cover, and cook an additional 10 minutes or until rice is fully cooked and liquid has been absorbed. (Cooking times for wild rice can vary greatly.) Season to taste with salt and pepper. Stir in pecans and parsley.

Meanwhile, drain the cranberries in the ramekin, discarding the brandy, and mince. Place in a small bowl and add the minced sage, rosemary, and thyme. Mix in the softened butter and season with salt and pepper. Gently loosen the skin on the hen halves and spread the butter mixture underneath with your fingers. Sprinkle hens all over with salt and pepper.

In the reserved skillet heat 1 tablespoon oil over medium-high heat. Add the hens, skin side down, and cook until nicely browned, about 5–7 minutes. Turn hens and place skillet in the oven. Roast for 25 minutes or until cooked through. Temperature should be 165° in thigh. Remove from oven and let rest 5 minutes.

Divide pilaf among 4 dinner plates. Arrange a hen half alongside and garnish plates with herb sprigs if desired. Serves 4.

Classic Combo

Cherry & Herb Game Hens with Smashed Potatoes
- *Replace rice pilaf with Pancetta & Leek Smashed Potatoes (page 230).*
- *Make herb butter, as above, replacing the cranberries with dried cherries and omitting the sage.*
- *Serve with either of the Cherry-Port Sauces (pages 92–93) if desired.*

Daring Pairing

Ginger & Lemongrass Infused Game Hens with Sweet Potatoes
- *Replace rice pilaf with Ginger & Sesame Twice-Baked Sweet Potatoes (page 233).*
- *Omit brandy, cranberries, and herbs.*
- *Combine softened butter with 2 tablespoons dark miso and 1 tablespoon each minced fresh ginger, garlic, and lemongrass.*

Goat Cheese–Stuffed Turkey Burgers with Charred Pepper & Onion Relish

Experimenting with burgers is fun, and it always leads to exciting new combinations, such as these delicious stuffed turkey burgers. The burgers can be shaped and refrigerated early in the day, leaving you nothing to do at dinnertime but grill them, along with the peppers and onions for the relish.

BURGERS

$1^1/_4$ POUND PACKAGE GROUND TURKEY (NOT EXTRA LEAN)

$^1/_4$ CUP DRY BREADCRUMBS

$^1/_4$ CUP CHOPPED FRESH CILANTRO

1 EGG, LIGHTLY BEATEN

1 TABLESPOON WORCESTERSHIRE SAUCE

2 TEASPOONS MINCED FRESH GARLIC

$1^1/_2$ TEASPOONS GOUND CUMIN

1 TEASPOON COARSE SALT

$^1/_2$ TEASPOON CRACKED PEPPER

$^1/_2$ TEASPOON MINCED LEMON ZEST

$^1/_4$ TEASPOON GROUND CAYENNE

3 TO 4 OUNCES SOFT FRESH GOAT CHEESE, FORMED INTO 4 DISKS, ABOUT $1^1/_2$ INCHES IN DIAMETER

CHARRED PEPPER & ONION RELISH

1 MEDIUM SWEET ONION, THICKLY SLICED

1 LARGE RED BELL PEPPER, QUARTERED, SEEDS AND VEINS REMOVED

1 LARGE YELLOW BELL PEPPER, QUARTERED, SEEDS AND VEINS REMOVED

2 TO 3 TABLESPOONS OLIVE OIL

2 TEASPOONS BALSAMIC VINEGAR

1 TEASPOON ROASTED GARLIC (PAGE 8 OR STORE-BOUGHT) OR $^1/_2$ TEASPOON MINCED FRESH GARLIC

1 TEASPOON SUGAR

1 TEASPOON GROUND CORIANDER

$^1/_4$ TEASPOON GROUND CAYENNE, OR TO TASTE SEA SALT AND FRESHLY GROUND PEPPER TO TASTE

4 LARGE ONION BUNS OR KAISER ROLLS, SPLIT OLIVE OIL

2 CUPS ARUGULA LEAVES, TRIMMED (OPTIONAL)

Preheat grill to medium-high heat. In a large bowl combine the turkey, breadcrumbs, cilantro, egg, Worcestershire, garlic, cumin, salt, pepper, lemon zest, and cayenne and mix well. Form into 8 patties. Place 1 disk of goat cheese in the middle of 4 patties and top with the remaining 4 patties. Seal edges well. Refrigerate while preparing the relish.

Brush onion slices and peppers with oil, season lightly with salt and pepper, and place directly on grill rack, or on perforated grill pan. (If not using a grill pan, thread onion slices onto long metal skewers to keep them together.) Grill the vegetables until softened and slightly charred, about 15 minutes, turning and moving around grill as needed. Remove from grill, let cool slightly, and chop roughly. In a medium bowl combine the chopped onion and peppers with the balsamic, garlic, sugar, coriander, cayenne, and salt and pepper and set aside.

Grill burgers over medium-high heat for 6 minutes, uncovered. Flip burgers, cover grill, and cook for 6 more minutes. Remove cover and cook for 2 more minutes or until no longer pink inside. During last 2 minutes of grilling, brush the cut sides of the buns with a little olive oil and place along outer edges of grill to toast lightly.

Divide arugula between bottom halves of buns; top with a burger and some of the relish. Pass remaining relish separately. Serves 4.

CLASSIC COMBO

Southwest Turkey Burgers with Guacamole
- *Increase cumin in burgers to 2½ teaspoons and replace lemon zest with lime zest.*
- *Replace goat cheese with 1 cup shredded pepper-jack cheese or Cheddar cheese.*
- *Replace relish with Guacamole (page 63).*
- *Omit arugula. Spread bottom half of buns with mayonnaise.*

DARING PAIRING

Mozzarella Turkey Burgers with Eggplant-Pepper Topping
- *Repalce cilantro with Italian parsley.*
- *Omit cumin and cayenne.*
- *Add 1 teaspoon dried oregano and ½ teaspoon dried thyme to burger mixture.*
- *Replace goat cheese with 1 cup shredded mozzarella cheese.*
- *Replace relish with Roasted Eggplant-Pepper Tapenade or Roasted Eggplant-Pepper Caponata (pages 80–81).*

PORK

Pork is delicious, versatile, and the way pigs are raised these days . . . lean. The recipes here are incredibly flavorful, incorporating a variety of marinades, stuffings, salsas and more. When cooking lean cuts such as tenderloin and chops; take great care not to overcook them. The internal temperature should be between 145° and 150°, nice and rosy in the center. If you don't have an instant-read thermometer, get out there and buy one. Also, be sure to let the meat rest for at least 5 minutes before slicing or you'll lose all those delicious juices to the cutting board . . . yikes!

Thai Lemongrass Grilled Pork Tenderloin with Cucumber-Pineapple Salsa

Pork tenderloin is so versatile. It tastes great combined with a wide variety of flavors, as you'll see in the recipes here.

THAI LEMONGRASS MARINADE

3   TABLESPOONS CHOPPED SCALLIONS

2   TABLESPOONS CHOPPED LEMONGRASS, INNER BULB ONLY

1½ TABLESPOONS CHOPPED FRESH GINGER

1½ TABLESPOONS CHOPPED FRESH GARLIC

2   TABLESPOONS SOY SAUCE

2   TABLESPOONS THAI OR VIETNAMESE FISH SAUCE

2   TABLESPOONS FRESH LIME JUICE

1½ TABLESPOONS LIGHT BROWN SUGAR

1   TABLESPOON ASIAN SESAME OIL

½   TABLESPOON ASIAN CHILE SAUCE

¼   CUP CHOPPED FRESH CILANTRO

2   PORK TENDERLOINS, ABOUT ¾ POUND EACH, TRIMMED OF EXCESS FAT AND SILVERSKIN

CUCUMBER-PINEAPPLE SALSA

1½ CUPS SEEDED, DICED CUCUMBER

¾   CUP DICED FRESH PINEAPPLE

4   SCALLIONS, MINCED, WHITE AND LIGHT GREEN PARTS ONLY

     GRATED ZEST OF 1 LIME

1½ TABLESPOONS FRESH LIME JUICE

2   TABLESPOONS SEASONED RICE VINEGAR

2   TEASPOONS ASIAN SESAME OIL

1½ TEASPOONS SOY SAUCE

1   TABLESPOON TOASTED SESAME SEEDS

3   TABLESPOONS MINCED FRESH CILANTRO

¾   TEASPOON ASIAN CHILE GARLIC SAUCE

SEA SALT AND FRESHLY GROUND PEPPER
CILANTRO SPRIGS FOR GARNISH

In a blender or mini-processor combine the marinade ingredients. Purée. Pour into a large ziplock bag, add the pork, and refrigerate for 2–3 hours, turning occasionally.

In a large bowl combine all salsa ingredients. Mix thoroughly and refrigerate until needed.

Preheat the grill to medium-high heat. Remove pork from marinade, pat dry, and season lightly with salt and pepper. Grill pork over direct heat until internal temperature reaches 145–150° about 13–15 minutes. Remove to a cutting board and let rest 5 minutes. Cut diagonally into ½-inch slices.

Fan pork slices out onto dinner plates and spoon salsa alongside, using a slotted spoon. Garnish with cilantro sprigs if desired. Serves 4–5.

NOTES

Pork can also be broiled, about 6 inches from the flame. Watch carefully and turn frequently.

CLASSIC COMBO

Jamaican Jerk Pork Tenderloin with Mango, Papaya & Roasted Red Pepper Salsa
- *Replace marinade with Jamaican Jerk Marinade (page 32).*
- *Replace salsa with Mango, Papaya & Roasted Red Pepper Salsa (page 70).*
- *Garnish with cilantro and/or thyme sprigs.*

DARING PAIRINGS

Orange Infused Pork Tenderloin with Cranberry-Port Sauce
- *Replace marinade with Red Wine-Orange Marinade (page 26)*
- *Replace salsa with Cranberry-Port Sauce, spooned atop pork (page 94)*
- *Garnish with thyme sprigs.*

Provençal Pork Tenderloin with Roasted Ratatouille Relish
- *Replace marinade with Provencal Herb Marinade (page 31)*
- *Replace salsa with Roasted Ratatouille Relish (page 82)*
- *Garnish with rosemary, thyme and/or tarragon sprigs.*

SEED CRUSTED PORK TENDERLOIN WITH ORANGE ROMESCO SAUCE

All of the recipes here can be completely prepared up to 8 hours ahead. Refrigerate the sauce and rewarm over gentle heat before serving. Brown the pork tenderloins; cool; wrap in plastic and refrigerate. Remove from the refrigerator 30–60 minutes before roasting; place on a baking sheet and roast as directed below.

ORANGE ROMESCO SAUCE

1   CUP FRESH ORANGE JUICE
1   BAY LEAF (MEDITERRANEAN)
1   CUP CHOPPED ROASTED RED BELL PEPPERS (PAGE 9 OR STORE-BOUGHT)
2   TABLESPOONS MINCED SHALLOT
2   TABLESPOONS TOMATO PASTE
1/4 CUP WALNUT OIL
1   TABLESPOON SHERRY VINEGAR
1/2 TEASPOON SPANISH SMOKED PAPRIKA (PIMENTÓN)
1   TABLESPOON UNSALTED BUTTER
    SEA SALT AND FRESHLY GROUND PEPPER

MEDITERRANEAN SEED CRUST

1   TABLESPOON LIGHTLY CRUSHED CORIANDER SEEDS

2   TEASPOONS LIGHTLY CRUSHED FENNEL SEEDS
1   TEASPOON LIGHTLY CRUSHED CUMIN SEEDS
1   TEASPOON COARSE SEA SALT OR KOSHER SALT
1/2 TEASPOON FRESHLY GROUND PEPPER
1/2 TEASPOON DRIED OREGANO (GREEK OR TURKISH PREFERRED)

2   PORK TENDERLOINS, ABOUT 3/4 POUND EACH, TRIMMED OF EXCESS FAT AND SILVERSKIN
2   TABLESPOONS OLIVE OIL
1/4 CUP TOASTED WALNUTS (OPTIONAL)

Preheat oven to 400°. Make sauce. Place orange juice and bay leaf in a medium saucepan and bring to a boil over medium-high heat. Boil gently until reduced to 1/2 cup, about 10 minutes. Add red peppers, shallot, and tomato paste, whisking to incorporate tomato paste, and boil for 5 minutes longer.

Carefully transfer orange juice mixture to a processor or blender. Add walnut oil, sherry vinegar, and paprika and purée. Return mixture to saucepan, whisk in 1 tablespoon butter, and season to taste with salt and pepper. Keep warm over low heat.

In a small bowl combine the seed crust ingredients and mix well. Use fingers to spread mixture all over tenderloins.

In a large nonstick ovenproof skillet heat 2 tablespoons olive oil over medium-high heat. Add pork and brown on all sides, about 6 minutes. Place skillet in oven and roast pork until internal temperature reaches 145–150°, about 12–15 minutes. Remove pork to cutting board and allow to rest for 5 minutes.

Slice pork into ¹/₂-inch thick slices and fan out on platter or plates. Spoon sauce over and sprinkle with walnut pieces. Pass remaining sauce separately. Serves 4–5.

CLASSIC COMBO

Herb Crusted Pork Tenderloin with Mushroom & Onion Sauce
- *Replace sauce with Sherried Mushroom & Caramelized Onion Sauce (page 106).*
- *Replace seed crust with 2¹/₂ tablespoons Savory Herb Rub (page 38).*
- *Omit walnuts. Garnish with chopped flat leaf parsley if desired.*

DARING PAIRINGS

Rosemary-Thyme Pork Tenderloin with Cherry-Port Sauce
- *Replace sauce with Cherry-Port Sauce with Pancetta & Wild Mushrooms (page 93).*
- *Replace seed crust with 2 tablespoons minced fresh rosemary, 1 tablespoon minced fresh thyme, 1 teaspoon coarse salt and ¹/₂ teaspoon pepper.*
- *Omit walnuts.*

Herb Crusted Pork Tenderloin with Roasted Garlic, Red Wine & Pepper Sauce
- *Replace sauce with Roasted Garlic, Red Wine & Pepper Sauce (page 99).*
- *Replace seed crust with 2¹/₂ tablespoons Savory Herb Rub (page 38).*
- *Omit walnuts.*

Mushroom Stuffed Pork Tenderloin with an Herbed Breadcrumb Crust

This is an impressive and delicious dinner party entrée that can be prepped well in advance. Stuff the tenderloins early in the day, wrap in plastic and refrigerate. Bread the tenderloins up to an hour before cooking and leave at room temperature.

Mushroom stuffing

$1/2$	TABLESPOON OLIVE OIL
2	OUNCES PANCETTA, CHOPPED
2	TABLESPOONS MINCED SHALLOTS
$1/2$	TABLESPOON MINCED FRESH GARLIC
$1/2$	POUND CREMINI MUSHROOMS, HALVED AND THINLY SLICED
$1/4$	POUND SHIITAKE MUSHROOMS, CAPS HALVED IF LARGE AND THINLY SLICED
1	TABLESPOON MINCED FRESH THYME
$1/4$	CUP DRY MARSALA OR SHERRY
$1/2$	CUP FRESH BREADCRUMBS
$1/2$	CUP GRATED FRESH PARMESAN CHEESE

SEA SALT AND FRESHLY GROUND PEPPER

3	CUPS FRESH BREADCRUMBS
$1/3$	CUP MINCED ITALIAN PARSLEY
4	GARLIC CLOVES, MINCED
$1^1/2$	TABLESPOONS MINCED FRESH ROSEMARY
$1/2$	TEASPOON GROUND BAY LEAVES
$1/2$	CUP FLOUR
1	EGG, LIGHTLY BEATEN
1	TABLESPOON UNSALTED BUTTER
2	TABLESPOONS OLIVE OIL

PARSLEY AND ROSEMARY SPRIGS FOR GARNISH

Pork and Breadcrumb Crust

2	PORK TENDERLOINS, ABOUT $3/4$ TO 1 POUND EACH

In a large skillet heat the olive oil over medium heat. Add pancetta and shallots and sauté for 4 minutes. Add garlic and sauté for 1 minute. Stir in mushrooms and thyme, cover pan, and cook for 3 minutes. Remove cover, increase heat to medium high, and sauté for an additional 8 minutes or until liquid has evaporated. Stir in Marsala and cook until evaporated, about 2 minutes. Stir in breadcrumbs and cook for an additional 2 minutes. Remove mixture to a bowl and stir in the Parmesan cheese. Cool slightly.

Preheat oven to 375°. Butterfly pork tenderloins by cutting horizontally through the center of each, leaving one long side attached. Open tenderloins out, like a book. Repeat procedure, cutting out from the center to the edges. Open flaps out and gently pound to an even $1/2$-inch thickness. Sprinkle with salt and pepper.

Spread mushroom mixture evenly over tenderloins, leaving a ½-inch border. Roll up tenderloins jellyroll-style and tie with kitchen string in four spots. Sprinkle outside of tenderloins with salt and pepper.

In a shallow bowl combine breadcrumbs, parsley, garlic, rosemary, and bay. Place flour and egg in separate shallow bowls. Coat tenderloins with flour, shaking off excess; dip in egg; coat in breadcrumbs.

In a large ovenproof, nonstick skillet melt butter in oil over medium-high heat. Add tenderloins and brown on all sides. Place skillet in oven and roast pork until thermometer inserted into center registers 148–150°, about 15–20 minutes. Remove to cutting board and let rest 5–10 minutes.

Slice tenderloins into ¾-inch slices, carefully remove strings and fan slices out onto plates or platter. Garnish with parsley and rosemary sprigs if desired. Serves 5–6.

CLASSIC COMBO

Florentine Pork Tenderloin
- *Omit mushroom stuffing.*
- *Butterfly tenderloins and sprinkle inside with pepper, but not salt.*
- *Top each tenderloin with 1 ounce thinly sliced prosciutto, ½ cup baby spinach leaves, ⅓ cup chopped roasted red peppers (page 9 or store-bought) and 1 cup freshly grated Parmesan cheese.*
- *Roll, tie, and proceed with recipe as directed.*

DARING PAIRING

Caponata Pork Involtini
   Replace mushroom stuffing with ½ recipe Roasted Eggplant-Pepper Caponata (page 81) plus ½ cup crumbled goat cheese.

Gruyère Stuffed Pork Chops with Spiced Apples

Pork chops have a reputation for being dry and leathery. The secret to these moist and delicious chops is a savory stuffing and taking care not to overcook them. I like the meatier flavor of bone-in chops, but you can substitute boneless loin chops if you prefer.

GRUYÈRE STUFFING

1 TABLESPOON UNSALTED BUTTER

2 OUNCES CHOPPED PANCETTA OR THICK-CUT BACON

1 MEDIUM LEEK, HALVED LENGTHWISE AND THINLY SLICED (ABOUT 1 CUP)

1/2 CUP FRESH BREADCRUMBS

1/4 CUP CHOPPED WALNUTS

1 TABLESPOON CHOPPED FRESH THYME

4 OUNCES FRESHLY GRATED GRUYÈRE CHEESE

4 12-OUNCE, 1 1/2-INCH THICK BONE-IN RIB LOIN PORK CHOPS

COARSE SALT AND FRESHLY GROUND PEPPER

2 TABLESPOONS OLIVE OIL

SPICED APPLES

2 TABLESPOONS UNSALTED BUTTER

1/2 CUP THINLY SLICED SHALLOTS

2 MEDIUM GRANNY SMITH APPLES, QUARTERED, CORED AND THINLY SLICED

1/4 TEASPOON GROUND CINNAMON

1/4 TEASPOON GROUND GINGER

1 CUP CHICKEN BROTH PLUS 1 TABLESPOON

1/3 CUP CALVADOS OR APPLE BRANDY

1/3 CUP APPLE CIDER

1 TEASPOON CORNSTARCH

1 TABLESPOON FRESH LEMON JUICE, OR MORE TO TASTE

SEA SALT AND FRESHLY CRACKED PEPPER

THYME SPRIGS FOR GARNISH

Preheat oven to 400°. In a large skillet melt 1 tablespoon butter over medium-high heat. Add pancetta and leek and sauté for 5 minutes. Add breadcrumbs, walnuts, and thyme and continue to sauté for 3 minutes. Remove to a bowl and stir in the Gruyère. Cool. Reserve skillet.

Cut a slit through the side of each pork chop, forming an internal pocket. Stuff the leek mixture into pockets, pressing opening closed to seal. Season outside of pork chops generously with salt and pepper.

In the reserved skillet heat 2 tablespoons olive oil over medium-high heat. Add chops and brown evenly, about 4 minutes per side. Transfer chops to a baking sheet and roast in the oven until internal temperature reaches 145°, about 6 minutes. Cover loosely with foil after removing from oven.

Meanwhile, in the same skillet melt 2 tablespoons butter over medium-high heat. Add shallots and apples and sauté for 5 minutes. Add cinnamon and ginger and sauté for 1 minute. Add 1 cup broth, Calvados, and cider, bring to a boil, and boil for 5 minutes. Whisk together cornstarch and remaining 1 tablespoon chicken broth and add to apples. Cook, stirring, for 2 minutes or until thickened. Remove from heat. Stir in lemon juice and season to taste with salt and pepper. Place chops on plates or platter and spoon sauce over. Garnish with thyme sprigs if desired. Serves 4.

Classic Combo

Gorgonzola Stuffed Pork Chops with Pears
- *Replace walnuts with pecans.*
- *Replace Gruyère with Gorgonzola (optional).*
- *Replace apples with 2 firm, ripe pears.*
- *Replace cinnamon and ginger with 2 teaspoons minced fresh rosemary.*
- *Replace Calvados and cider with ⅔ cup tawny port.*
- *Replace lemon juice with Dijon mustard.*

Daring Pairing

Sicilian Style Chops with Orange & Fennel
- *Replace walnuts with pine nuts, unchopped.*
- *Replace Gruyère with Parmesan or Asiago.*
- *Place 2 thin orange slices, unpeeled, under each pork chop prior to placing in the oven.*
- *Replace apples with 1 large fennel bulb, thinly sliced.*
- *Replace cinnamon and ginger with ½ tablespoon minced fresh thyme and ½ teaspoon dried oregano.*
- *Replace Calvados with dry Marsala.*
- *Replace cider with fresh orange juice.*
- *Omit lemon juice.*
- *Sprinkle finished dish with 2 tablespoons chopped fennel fronds.*

Hoisin Braised Pork with Mushrooms

Braised dishes are the ultimate comfort food for a cold winter's night. Long, slow cooking turns this economical cut of pork into a luscious main dish. You may want to make this dish on a lazy Sunday afternoon to serve on a hectic weeknight. Cool, cover, and refrigerate for up to 2 days (the flavors keep getting better) or freeze for up to 3 months. I like to serve this dish in large, shallow pasta bowls, with a big scoop of mashed potatoes alongside to soak up the flavorful gravy.

1   OUNCE DRIED PORCINI MUSHROOMS

$3/4$ CUP BOILING WATER

2   POUNDS BONELESS PORK SHOULDER OR
    BONELESS PORK COUNTRY-STYLE SPARERIBS,
    CUT INTO $1^1/2$-INCH PIECES
    SEA SALT AND FRESHLY GROUND PEPPER

4   TABLESPOONS OLIVE OIL, DIVIDED

$1^1/4$ CUPS LOW SODIUM CHICKEN BROTH OR
    HOMEMADE STOCK, DIVIDED

1   LARGE SWEET ONION, THINLY SLICED

1   TABLESPOON MINCED FRESH GARLIC

1   TABLESPOON MINCED FRESH GINGER

8   OUNCES SHIITAKE MUSHROOMS, CAPS
    THINLY SLICED

1   BUNCH SCALLIONS, THINLY SLICED

3   TABLESPOONS FLOUR

1   POUND CARROTS, PEELED AND CUT
    DIAGONALLY INTO $1/2$-INCH THICK SLICES

1   CUP APPLE CIDER

$1/3$ CUP HOISIN SAUCE

2   TABLESPOONS SOY SAUCE

1   CINNAMON STICK

1   STAR ANISE POD (OPTIONAL)

$1/3$ CUP ROUGHLY CHOPPED, SALTED CASHEWS

Preheat oven to 350°. Combine porcinis and boiling water in a small bowl, cover with plastic wrap and set aside.

Sprinkle pork generously with salt and pepper. In a large Dutch oven or other heavy, ovenproof pot heat 2 tablespoons oil over medium-high heat. Add half of the pork and cook until pieces are well browned on all sides, about 10 minutes. Remove pork to a plate, add 1 tablespoon oil to pot and repeat with remaining pork. Remove pork to plate.

Add $1/4$ cup chicken broth to pot and scrape up browned bits. Add remaining 1 tablespoon oil to the pot; then add the onions, cover, and cook for 3 minutes. Uncover and sauté until onions are softenend and lightly browned, about 8 minutes.

Meanwhile, remove porcini mushrooms from liquid with a slotted spoon and chop. Reserve liquid.

Clear a spot in the center of the onions and add the garlic and ginger. Cook for 1 minute. Add the porcini mushrooms, shiitake mushrooms, and half of the scallions and sauté for 2 minutes. Sprinkle the flour over the vegetables and cook, stirring, for 2 minutes.

Return pork, along with any accumulated juices, to pot and stir in remaining 1 cup chicken broth, carrots, apple cider, hoisin sauce, soy sauce, cinnamon stick, star anise pod, and reserved porcini liquid, taking care to leave behind any sediment.

Bring mixture to a boil, cover with a tight fitting lid, and place in the oven to braise for 1 hour. Check after 15 minutes to make sure mixture is at a steady simmer.

Remove from oven, season with salt and pepper as desired, and sprinkle with remaining scallions and cashews. Serves 6.

CLASSIC COMBO

Orange & Fennel Braised Pork
- *Omit porcini mushrooms and boiling water.*
- *Sprinkle pork with 2 teaspoons ground coriander and 2 teaspoons ground fennel, along with the salt and pepper.*
- *Add 1 large, thinly sliced fennel bulb, along with the onion.*
- *Omit shiitake mushrooms and scallions.*
- *Replace apple cider with 1 cup fresh orange juice, the grated zest of 1 orange and 1/2 cup medium dry sherry (such as Amontillado.)*
- *Add 1/2 cup medium dry sherry (such as Amontillado), along with the other liquids.*
- *Omit hoisin sauce and star anise.*
- *After removing pot from oven, stir in 1 tablespoon sherry vinegar.*
- *Sprinkle with 2 tablespoons chopped fennel fronds if desired.*

DARING PAIRINGS

Pork Braised with Port & Figs
- *Sprinkle pork with 1 teaspoon dried, thyme, 1 teaspoon ground sage and 1/2 teaspoon dry mustard, along with salt and pepper.*
- *Omit ginger and scallions.*
- *Replace shiitake mushrooms with cremini mushrooms.*
- *Add 1 cup quartered dried figs and 2 bay leaves, along with carrots.*
- *Replace apple cider with 1 cup tawny port.*
- *Omit hoisin sauce, cinnamon stick, star anise and cashews.*
- *After removing pot from oven, stir in 1–2 tablespoons balsamic vinegar.*
- *Sprinkle with 1/4 cup minced Italian parsley.*

Jambalaya Burgers with Roasted Red Pepper Remoulade

Ground pork makes for juicy and delicious burgers, particularly when combined with spicy sausages and seasonings, as these are. All of the burgers here can be prepped, and the toppings made, up to 4 hours in advance.

ROASTED RED PEPPER REMOULADE

$^1/_2$ CUP CHOPPED ROASTED RED PEPPER (PAGE 9 OR STORE-BOUGHT), PATTED DRY

$^1/_2$ CUP MAYONNAISE

3 TABLESPOONS MINCED CELERY

2 TABLESPOONS MINCED FRESH ITALIAN PARSLEY

1 TABLESPOON MINCED SHALLOT

1 TABLESPOON CREOLE MUSTARD

1 TABLESPOON PREPARED OR CREAM-STYLE HORSERADISH

1 TABLESPOON WORCESTERSHIRE SAUCE

1 TEASPOON MINCED FRESH GARLIC

$^1/_2$ TEASPOON LOUISIANA-STYLE HOT SAUCE

JAMBALAYA BURGERS

2 POUNDS GROUND PORK

8 OUNCES FULLY COOKED ANDOUILLE SAUSAGE, FINELY CHOPPED

$^1/_2$ CUP MINCED ONION

$^1/_2$ CUP MINCED GREEN BELL PEPPER

3 TABLESPOONS CAJUN-CREOLE SPICE RUB (PAGE 34 OR STORE-BOUGHT)

2 TABLESPOONS WORCESTERSHIRE SAUCE

1 TABLESPOON MINCED FRESH GARLIC

1 TABLESPOON MINCED JALAPEÑO PEPPER

6 LARGE ONION BUNS

LETTUCE LEAVES (OPTIONAL)

SWEET PICKLE SLICES (OPTIONAL)

In a mini-processor combine all remoulade ingredients and purée to a slightly chunky sauce. Remove to a small bowl and refrigerate until needed.

Preheat grill to medium-high heat. In a large bowl, thoroughly combine all burger ingredients and shape into 6 1-inch-thick patties.

Oil grill grate. Grill burgers over direct heat for about 7 minutes per side, or until cooked through to an internal temperature of 150°. Remove burgers. Grill buns, cut side down, until toasted, about 2 minutes.

Spread some remoulade on the bottom half of each bun; top with lettuce leaves, a burger, more remoulade, pickles and top of bun. Serves 6.

NOTES

- Use uncooked andouille sausage if preferred. Squeeze from casings and combine with pork mixture. Increase cooking time slightly. If outside of burgers char, move to a cooler part of the grill, cover and cook until done.

- Burgers can also be broiled or cooked atop the stove in a ridged grill pan or on a griddle.
- If using a purchased Cajun-Creole spice blend, be sure to check the salt level and package directions, and adjust accordingly.

CLASSIC COMBO

Jerk Pork Burgers with Grilled Pineapple and Mojo Mayo
- *Replace remoulade with Mojo Mayo (page 44).*
- *Omit sausage from burgers.*
- *Replace Cajun seasoning with 4 tablespoons Jamaican Jerk Spice Rub (page 32 or store-bought).*
- *Increase jalapeño to 2 tablespoons (optional).*
- *Replace pickles with fresh or canned pineapple rings, grilled.*

DARING PAIRING

Spanish-Spiced Burgers with Romesco Mayo
- *Replace remoulade with Romesco Mayo (page 44).*
- *Replace andouille sausage with chorizo sausage, cooked or fresh.*
- *Replace Cajun seasoning with 2 teaspoons Spanish smoked paprika (pimentón), 1 teaspoon ground cumin, 1/2 teaspoon dried thyme, 1/2 teaspoon dried oregano, 2 teaspoons coarse salt and 1 teaspoon cracked pepper.*
- *Replace jalapeño with 1/4 cup minced Italian parsley.*
- *Omit pickles.*

BEEF AND LAMB

The recipes in this chapter run the gamut from juicy grilled steaks and lamb chops to inventive burgers, hearty braises, and succulent roasts.

Many of the recipes here are great for entertaining, as they can be prepped well in advance. In addition, cuts such as flank steak and sirloin are affordable and offer rich, beefy flavor.

Lamb is the darling of many restaurant chefs, but it can be easily prepared, with equally delicious results, in your own kitchen. Be sure to buy only the freshest lamb, from a reliable butcher.

Rosemary Grilled Rib-Eyes with Gorgonzola-Walnut Butter

You'll think you're at the best steakhouse in town after the first bite of these scrumptious steaks! Keep some of the flavored butter stashed in the freezer and dinner can be on the table in less than an hour.

Gorgonzola-Walnut Butter

1 stick unsalted butter, softened
1/3 cup crumbled Gorgonzola cheese
1/4 cup chopped walnuts, lightly toasted
1/2 teaspoon Hungarian sweet paprika
1/2 teaspoon freshly ground pepper
1/4 teaspoon sea salt

Rosemary Grilled Rib-Eyes

2 to 2 1/2 pounds boneless rib-eye steaks, about 1–1 1/4 inches thick
2 tablespoons olive oil
2 tablespoons minced fresh rosemary
1 tablespoon coarse salt
1 tablespoon coarsely ground pepper

Rosemary sprigs for garnish

In a small bowl thoroughly mix all butter ingredients. Scrape out onto a sheet of plastic wrap and form mixture into a log, about 6 inches long, wrapping tightly. Refrigerate until firm, at least 1 hour or up to 3 days. Cut into 1/4-inch slices to use.

Rub steaks with oil. In a small bowl combine rosemary, salt, and pepper and rub over steaks. Let stand for at least 30 minutes, or refrigerate for up to 2 hours.

Preheat grill to medium-high heat. Oil grill grates. Grill steaks over direct heat for about 4–5 minutes per side for medium rare, turning every 2 minutes and moving to a cooler part of the grill if the outside is charring too quickly. Remove to a cutting board; top with about half of the Gorgonzola-Walnut Butter slices; cover loosely with foil and let rest for 5 minutes. Slice steaks into 1/3-inch thick slices; transfer to platter and serve. Garnish with rosemary sprigs. Pass additional butter slices separately. Serves 4.

Notes

Steaks can also be broiled or seared in a hot pan and finished in a 375° oven.

Classic Combo

Rosemary Grilled Rib-Eyes with Balsamic-Gorgonzola Onions
- *Omit Gorgonzola-Walnut Butter.*
- *Top sliced steaks with Balsamic-Gorgonzola Onions (page 78).*

Daring Pairings

Grilled Rib-Eyes with Smoked Paprika & Roasted Garlic Butter
- *Replace Gorgonzola-Walnut Butter with Smoked Paprika & Roasted Garlic Butter (page 52).*
- *Replace half of the minced rosemary with minced fresh thyme.*

Bourbon-Molasses Rib-Eyes with Smoky Chipotle Butter
- *Replace Gorgonzola-Walnut Butter with Smoky Chipotle Butter (page 52).*
- *Omit rosemary.*
- *Brush steaks with Bourbon-Molasses Glaze (page 122) during the second half of grilling.*

Pan-Roasted Sirloin with Vegetable Relish & Tomato-Basil Butter

This recipe is, admittedly, a bit over-the-top. You can certainly make either the butter or the relish, rather than both, but the combination is phenomenal. If you keep a Tomato-Basil Butter "log" in the freezer, as I do, preparing this dish is a breeze!

Balsamic Marinade and Steak

1/2 CUP BALSAMIC VINEGAR

1/2 CUP EXTRA VIRGIN OLIVE OIL

1/2 CUP MINCED SHALLOTS

2 TABLESPOONS MINCED FRESH ROSEMARY

1 TABLESPOON MINCED FRESH THYME

1/2 TEASPOON COARSE SALT

1/2 TEASPOON FRESHLY GROUND PEPPER

2 POUNDS BONELESS TOP SIRLOIN STEAKS, ABOUT 1-INCH THICK, OR NEW YORK STRIP STEAKS

Tomato-Basil Butter

1/2 STICK UNSALTED BUTTER, SOFTENED

2 SUN-DRIED TOMATO HALVES, PACKED IN OIL, DRAINED, MINCED

1 1/2 TABLESPOONS MINCED FRESH BASIL

1/2 TABLESPOON DOUBLE CONCENTRATED TOMATO PASTE (OR 1 TABLESPOON REGULAR TOMATO PASTE)

Vegetable Relish

1 MEDIUM EGGPLANT, UNPEELED AND CUT INTO 1/2-INCH CHUNKS (ABOUT 4 CUPS)

8 OUNCES CREMINI MUSHROOMS, QUARTERED

1 MEDIUM RED BELL PEPPER, CUT INTO 1/2-INCH CHUNKS

1 MEDIUM YELLOW BELL PEPPER, CUT INTO 1/2-INCH CHUNKS

1 LARGE SWEET ONION, CUT INTO 1/2-INCH CHUNKS

1/4 CUP EXTRA VIRGIN OLIVE OIL

1 1/2 TABLESPOONS PESTO (PAGE 104 OR STORE-BOUGHT)

1 TABLESPOON ROASTED GARLIC (PAGE 8 OR STORE-BOUGHT)

SEA SALT AND FRESHLY GROUND PEPPER

2 TABLESPOONS OLIVE OIL

ROSEMARY AND THYME SPRIGS FOR GARNISH

In a medium bowl whisk together all marinade ingredients. Place in a ziplock plastic bag along with steaks and marinate, refrigerated, for 2–4 hours. Remove from refrigerator 30–60 minutes before cooking.

Meanwhile, make Tomato-Basil Butter. In a small bowl mash together all butter ingredients. Season to taste with salt and pepper. Scrape out onto a sheet of plastic wrap and form mixture into a log, wrapping tightly. Refrigerate until firm, at least 1 hour.

Preheat oven to 400°. To make vegetable relish, place eggplant, mushrooms, bell peppers, and onion on a large, heavy baking sheet or roasting pan. Drizzle with olive oil and toss well to coat evenly. Sprinkle generously with salt and pepper. Roast in the center of the oven for 20 minutes. Remove pan, stir, return to oven, and roast for an additional 25 minutes or until vegetables are soft and beginning to brown. Remove mixture to a large bowl and mash lightly with a potato masher. Stir in pesto and garlic.

Drain steak, discarding marinade, and pat dry. Season with salt and pepper. In a large, ovenproof skillet heat 2 tablespoons olive oil over medium-high heat. Add steak and sear for 4 minutes. Turn steaks, place pan in oven, and roast for about 5 minutes for medium rare, or to desired degree of doneness. Remove steak to cutting board, top with $1/4$-inch thick slices of Tomato-Basil Butter, tent loosely with foil and allow to rest for 5 minutes.

Slice steaks into $1/3$-inch thick slices. Divide vegetable relish between plates and fan steak slices over. Garnish plates with herb sprigs if desired. Serves 4.

CLASSIC COMBO

Scarborough Sirloin with Wild Mushrooms & Onion Jam
- *Replace marinade with Scarborough Fair Marinade (page 27).*
- *Omit butter and vegetable relish.*
- *Top steak slices with Wild Mushroom Sauté (page 86) and Sweet & Savory Onion Jam (page 78).*

DARING PAIRINGS

Basil-Balsamic Sirloin with Aioli
- *Replace marinade with Basil-Balsamic Marinade (page 24).*
- *Omit butter and vegetable relish.*
- *Top steak slices with Sun-Dried Tomato and Basil Aioli (page 48)*

Sicilian Sirloin
- *Replace marinade with Orange-Balsamic Marinade (page 24).*
- *Omit butter and vegetable relish.*
- *Top steak slices with Roasted Eggplant-Pepper Caponata (page 81).*

Teriyaki Sirloin with Coconut-Corn Salsa
- *Replace marinade with Teriyaki Marinade (page 16).*
- *Omit butter and vegetable relish.*
- *Fan steak slices on a bed of Coconut-Corn Salsa (page 64).*

Argentine Flank Steak with Chimichurri Sauce

Beef is big in Argentina, and the pungent parsley-garlic sauce called chimichurri is frequently served alongside. This version is exceptionally delicious . . . especially if you're a garlic lover!

Chimichurri Sauce

2   cups Italian parsley leaves, packed
6   cloves garlic, chopped
4   scallions, chopped
$^1/_2$ cup extra virgin olive oil
$^1/_4$ cup red wine vinegar
1   tablespoon fresh lime juice
2   teaspoons dried oregano
$^1/_2$ to 1 teaspoon red pepper flakes
    Sea salt and freshly ground pepper

Flank Steak

3   tablespoons Southwest Spice Rub (page 34 or store-bought)
1   teaspoon dried oregano
$^1/_2$ teaspoon rubbed sage
$^1/_2$ teaspoon cayenne pepper
1   1$^1/_2$ to 2 pound flank steak, trimmed

Italian parsley sprigs and lime wedges for garnish

Preheat grill to medium-high heat.

Make sauce. In a food processor combine the parsley, garlic, scallions, olive oil, vinegar, lime juice, oregano, and red pepper flakes. Process until fairly smooth. Season to taste with salt and pepper. Refrigerate, covered, until needed.

In a small bowl combine Southwest Spice Rub, oregano, sage, and cayenne and rub all over flank steak.

Oil grill grates and grill steak, over direct heat, 4 minutes per side for medium rare. Remove steak to a cutting board, tent loosely with foil, and allow to rest for 5 minutes.

Thinly slice steak, across the grain, and fan out on platter or plates. Spoon some of the chimichurri sauce over the steak, passing the remaining sauce separately. Garnish with parsley sprigs and lime wedges if desired. Serves 4.

NOTES

- This steak may also be broiled, or seared in a hot pan and finished in a 375° oven.
- If using a purchased spice blend, be sure to check the salt level and package directions, and adjust accordingly.

CLASSIC COMBO

Southwest Spiced Flank Steak with Pancetta-Corn Salsa
- *Omit chimichurri.*
- *Rub steak with Southwest Spice Rub, omitting additional oregano, sage, and cayenne.*
- *Serve sliced steak atop a bed of Pancetta-Corn Salsa (page 60).*
- *Optional: Top the steak with slices of Cilantro-Lime Butter (page 56) or Smoky Chipotle Butter (page 52) while it rests.*

DARING PAIRINGS

Cajun Spiced Flank Steak with Sweet Corn Remoulade
- *Replace chimichurri with Sweet Corn Remoulade (page 50).*
- *Replace all spice rub ingredients with 3 tablespoons Cajun-Creole Spice Rub (page 34 or store-bought).*

Ancho-Cinnamon Flank Steak with Cherry-Port Sauce
- *Replace chimichurri with Cherry-Port Sauce (page 92).*
- *Replace all spice rub ingredients with 1 recipe Ancho-Cinnamon Spice Rub (page 36) plus an additional 1/2 teaspoon sea salt.*

Korean Beef & Pork Lettuce Wraps with Sesame-Soy Dipping Sauce

Lettuce wraps are a fun entrée for a casual party or weeknight dinner. These recipes call for half beef and half pork, but you can certainly use one or the other. Sliced chicken breasts or thighs would also be delicious in each of the variations.

Korean-Style BBQ Marinade

$^1/_3$ CUP SOY SAUCE

2   TABLESPOONS MIRIN

2   TABLESPOONS DARK BROWN SUGAR

2   TABLESPOONS MINCED FRESH GARLIC

$1^1/_2$ TABLESPOONS ASIAN SESAME OIL

$1^1/_2$ TABLESPOONS ASIAN CHILE SAUCE

1   TABLESPOON MINCED FRESH GINGER

$^3/_4$ POUND BEEF SIRLOIN OR TENDERLOIN STEAKS, THINLY SLICED AGAINST THE GRAIN

$^3/_4$ POUND PORK TENDERLOIN, HALVED LENGTHWISE AND THINLY SLICED AGAINST THE GRAIN

Sesame-Soy Dipping Sauce

$^2/_3$ CUP SOY SAUCE

6   TABLESPOONS SAKE OR DRY SHERRY

$^1/_4$ CUP SUGAR

8   SCALLIONS, MINCED, WHITE AND MOST OF GREEN PARTS

2   TABLESPOONS ASIAN SESAME OIL

2   TABLESPOONS TOASTED SESAME SEEDS

2   TEASPOONS RICE VINEGAR

3   TABLESPOONS TOASTED SESAME SEEDS

6   MINCED SCALLIONS, WHITE AND MOST OF GREEN PARTS

1   HEAD ROMAINE LETTUCE, LEAVES WASHED AND PATTED DRY
    STEAMED JASMINE RICE OR STICKY RICE (OPTIONAL)

In a medium bowl thoroughly whisk together all marinade ingredients, dissolving sugar. Divide the marinade between 2 ziplock bags. Add beef slices to one bag and pork slices to the other, coating thoroughly with marinade. Marinate meat, refrigerated, for 1–3 hours, turning bags occasionally.

Meanwhile, in a medium bowl whisk together dipping sauce ingredients, dissolving sugar. Refrigerate until needed.

Preheat the grill to medium-high heat. Remove meat from marinade, discarding marinade. Oil a grill basket or perforated grill pan. Preheat basket on grill for a minute or two. Place beef slices on basket and grill for about 4 minutes, flipping frequently, or to desired degree of doneness. Remove to a serving bowl. Repeat with pork slices. Remove to a separate serving bowl. Divide sesame seeds and minced scallions between beef and pork and stir to combine.

Place lettuce leaves on a plate and serve alongside bowls of beef, pork, and rice for wrapping. Divide dipping sauce between 4 individual bowls. Serves 4.

NOTES

- Meat is equally delicious sautéed in a hot skillet.
- For a spicier dish, whisk 2–3 tablespoons Asian chile sauce into dipping sauce.

CLASSIC COMBO

Thai Lemongrass Lettuce Wraps with Spicy Peanut Dipping Sauce
- *Replace marinade with Thai Lemongrass Marinade (page 14).*
- *Replace dipping sauce with Spicy Peanut Dipping Sauce (page 110).*
- *Omit toasted sesame seeds.*

DARING PAIRINGS

Thai Coconut Lettuce Wraps with Cucumber-Pineapple Salsa
- *Replace marinade with Thai Coconut Marinade (page 14).*
- *Dipping sauce is optional.*
- *Omit toasted sesame seeds and minced scallions.*
- *Serve Cucumber-Pineapple Salsa (page 66) as an additional filling.*

Teriyaki Lettuce Wraps with Wasabi Ponzu
- *Replace marinade with Teriyaki Marinade (page 16).*
- *Replace dipping sauce with Wasabi Ponzu (page 112).*
- *Omit toasted sesame seeds.*
- *Pineapple-Sesame Dipping Sauce (page 108) would also be great here.*

Jamaican Jerk Lettuce Wraps with Savory Mango-Papaya Salsa
- *Replace marinade with Jamaican Jerk Marinade (page 32).*
- *Omit dipping sauce, toasted sesame seeds, scallions and rice.*
- *Serve Savory Mango-Papaya Salsa (page 70) as an additional filling.*

HERBED FLANK STEAK ROULADE WITH RED PEPPER–WINE SAUCE

This could very well be the perfect dinner party entrée! It's beautiful, absolutely delicious, affordable and can be prepared in advance. If you don't want to butterfly the steak, your butcher should be happy to do it for you.

HERBED FLANK STEAK ROULADE

1   LARGE FLANK STEAK, ABOUT 1½ POUNDS

3   OUNCES THINLY SLICED PROSCIUTTO

1   CUP LOOSELY PACKED BASIL LEAVES

1   CUP FRESH BREAD CRUMBS

⅔   CUP FRESHLY GRATED PARMESAN CHEESE

¼   CUP CHOPPED ITALIAN PARSLEY, PLUS SPRIGS
     FOR GARNISH
     GRATED ZEST OF 1 LEMON

2   TABLESPOONS MINCED FRESH GARLIC,
     DIVIDED

5   TABLESPOONS EXTRA VIRGIN OLIVE OIL,
     DIVIDED

2   TABLESPOONS MINCED FRESH ROSEMARY

RED PEPPER–WINE SAUCE

3   TABLESPOONS UNSALTED BUTTER, DIVIDED

¾   CUP MINCED SHALLOTS

1   CUP CHOPPED ROASTED RED BELL PEPPERS
     (PAGE 9 OR STORE-BOUGHT)

1   CUP DRY RED WINE

1   CUP LOW SODIUM CHICKEN BROTH OR
     HOMEMADE STOCK

1   TABLESPOON BALSAMIC VINEGAR
     SEA SALT AND FRESHLY GROUND PEPPER

Preheat oven to 375°. Lay the flank steak on work surface with the grain running parallel to you. Butterfly the flank steak by slicing through it horizontally, leaving meat attached on back side. Open steak, like a book, flattening seam. Sprinkle cut surface with pepper. Lay prosciutto slices over surface of steak, leaving a ½-inch border on the back side. Scatter basil leaves evenly over prosciutto. In a medium bowl combine breadcrumbs, Parmesan cheese, parsley, lemon zest, 1 tablespoon garlic, and 2 tablespoons olive oil. Sprinkle this mixture evenly over basil and press down gently. Starting at edge closest to you, roll up steak tightly and tie with kitchen string in 4 or 5 places. Combine 2 tablespoons olive oil, remaining 1 tablespoon garlic, and rosemary and rub over the outside of the steak. Sprinkle with salt and pepper.

Heat the remaining 1 tablespoon olive oil in a large ovenproof skillet over medium high heat. Sear steak on all sides, about 6–8 minutes total. Place pan in oven and roast until internal temperature reaches 125°, about 20–25 minutes. Remove meat to a cutting board, tent loosely with foil, and let rest for 10 minutes.

While meat cooks and rests, make sauce. In a medium skillet heat 2 tablespoons butter over medium heat. Add shallots and sauté 5 minutes. Add bell pepper and sauté 3 minutes. Add wine; bring to a boil and boil gently for 5 minutes or until almost evaporated. Add broth; return to a boil and boil gently for 5 minutes. Carefully transfer mixture to blender or processor and purée. Return sauce to pan and whisk in remaining 1 tablespoon butter and balsamic. Season to taste with salt and pepper.

Spoon some sauce onto each dinner plate. Slice steak roll into $1/2$-inch thick slices, discarding strings. Place 2 slices on each plate, atop sauce. Garnish plates with parsley sprigs if desired. Pass remaining sauce separately. Serves 4.

Notes

Sauce and steak roulade can be prepared up to one day ahead and refrigerated, covered. Take meat out of refrigerator one hour before searing and roasting.

Classic Combos

Argentina-Style Flank Steak . . . Matambre
- *Replace basil leaves with $1/4$ cup fresh oregano leaves.*
- *Replace lemon zest with lime zest.*
- *Replace rosemary with 2 tablespoons crushed cumin seeds.*
- *Replace sauce with Chimichurri Sauce (page 104), spooned over steak slices.*

Daring Pairing

Korean BBQ Steak Roll
- *Marinade butterflied flank steak in Korean-Style BBQ Marinade (page 18) for 2–12 hours. Remove steak from marinade and pat dry with paper towels before proceeding with prosciutto layer. Reserve marinade. Replace basil leaves with baby spinach leaves.*
- *Omit all remaining ingredients (breadcrumbs through rosemary).*
- *Top spinach layer with 1 bunch minced scallions, 1 large carrot shredded into thin strips with a vegetable peeler and $1/2$ cup minced red bell pepper.*
- *Roll and tie as directed above. Rub outside of roll with 2 tablespoons peanut oil; sprinkle with salt and pepper; place on a heavy baking sheet and roast at 375° until internal temperature reaches 125°, about 30–35 minutes. Rest and slice as above. Omit sauce.*
- *Boil reserved marinade in a small saucepan for 2 minutes and drizzle over steak slices.*

BRAISED BEEF TOSCANA

It doesn't get any better than home-style braised beef on a cold winter's night. These recipes are perfect for a cozy fireside dinner with family or friends. Feel free to cook the entire dish a day or two in advance. It'll be even tastier as the meat absorbs more of the sauce while resting in the fridge! Just reheat and add the final garnishes right before serving.

$2^1/_2$ TO 3 POUNDS BEEF CHUCK, CUT INTO $1^1/_2$-INCH PIECES

2   TABLESPOONS MINCED FRESH ROSEMARY

2   TEASPOONS GROUND FENNEL SEED

$1^1/_2$ TEASPOONS COARSE SEA SALT OR KOSHER SALT

1   TEASPOON FRESHLY GROUND PEPPER

4   TO 6 TABLESPOONS OLIVE OIL, DIVIDED

3   CUPS CHOPPED SWEET ONION

1   CUP CHOPPED CARROT

1   LARGE RED BELL PEPPER, DICED

2   TABLESPOONS MINCED FRESH GARLIC

1   TABLESPOON DOUBLE CONCENTRATED TOMATO PASTE (OR 2 TABLESPOONS REGULAR)

$1^1/_4$ CUPS DRY RED WINE, SUCH AS CHIANTI, DIVIDED

$1/_4$ CUP FLOUR

1   15-OUNCE CAN DICED TOMATOES WITH ITALIAN HERBS, UNDRAINED

1   CUP BEEF BROTH

$1^1/_2$ TABLESPOONS WORCESTERSHIRE SAUCE

2   BAY LEAVES

3   THYME SPRIGS

3   OUNCES THINLY SLICED PROSCIUTTO, CUT INTO THIN STRIPS

1   MEDIUM EGGPLANT, CUT INTO $3/_4$-INCH PIECES

1   POUND CREMINI MUSHROOMS, THICKLY SLICED

$1/_4$ CUP CHOPPED ITALIAN PARSLEY

1   TABLESPOON BALSAMIC VINEGAR

Preheat oven to 400°. Sprinkle beef with rosemary, fennel, salt, and pepper. In a large, heavy Dutch oven heat 2 tablespoons olive oil over medium-high heat. Brown the meat in 2 or 3 batches, making sure not to crowd the pan. Remove meat to a bowl as each batch has browned nicely. Use 1–2 tablespoons additional oil as needed.

Add onion, carrot, red pepper, and garlic to the pan; reduce the heat to medium and sauté until the vegetables are soft, about 10 minutes, scraping up the browned bits from the bottom of the pan as the vegetables release their liquid. Stir in the tomato paste and about $1/_2$ cup of the wine and cook until the liquid has evaporated, about 2 minutes. Sprinkle the flour over the vegetables and cook, stirring, for 30 seconds. Add the remaining wine, tomatoes, broth, Worcestershire, bay leaves, thyme sprigs, beef, and any accumulated juices. Bring to a boil. Cover the pan with a tight fitting lid and place in the oven to braise for 1½ hours. Check after 10 minutes to make sure the liquid is at a steady simmer.

Meanwhile, heat the remaining 2 tablespoons olive oil in a large (12-inch) skillet over medium-high heat. Add the prosciutto and cook until crisp, about 5 minutes. With a slotted spoon remove prosciutto to a paper towel lined plate. Add eggplant and mushrooms to skillet and sauté until softened and lightly browned, about 15 minutes. Set aside.

Remove beef mixture from oven and stir in eggplant, mushrooms, and half of the parsley. Cover and let rest for 10 minutes. Uncover, stir in vinegar, and sprinkle with prosciutto and remaining parsley. Serve with Roasted Garlic Smashed Potatoes (page 230), egg noodles, or polenta if desired. Serves 6.

CLASSIC COMBO

Braised Beef Espana
- *Replace rosemary and fennel with 1 tablespoon Spanish smoked paprika (pimentón), 2 teaspoons dried oregano, and 2 teaspoons ground cumin.*
- *Replace red pepper with 1 green pepper plus 1–2 minced jalapeño peppers.*
- *Replace wine with dry (Fino or Manzanilla) sherry.*
- *Replace eggplant with 1 red bell pepper and 1 yellow bell pepper, cut into thin strips.*
- *Replace balsamic vinegar with sherry vinegar.*
- *Sprinkle toasted, sliced almonds over finished dish if desired.*
- *Serve with mashed potatoes, polenta, couscous or rice.*

DARING PAIRING

Orange-Hoisin Braised Beef
- *Replace rosemary and fennel with 1 teaspoon Chinese 5-Spice powder and 2 teaspoons ground coriander.*
- *Add 1 tablespoon minced fresh ginger along with the garlic.*
- *Replace the wine with fresh orange juice.*
- *Add ⅓ cup hoisin sauce along with liquid ingredients.*
- *Omit Worcestershire, thyme, prosciutto, eggplant and mushrooms.*
- *Add 1 pound carrots, peeled and sliced diagonally ½-inch thick, to the pot halfway through oven braising.*
- *Omit parsley and balsamic vinegar.*
- *Sprinkle ½ cup minced scallions over the finished dish if desired.*
- *Serve with mashed potatoes or rice.*

Indian-Spiced Burgers with Coconut-Cilantro Chutney & Grilled Pineapple

Your neighbors will come running when they catch the aroma of these burgers wafting from your grill! The spice combination is divine and the cooling chutney and sweet pineapple are the perfect complements.

Coconut-Cilantro Chutney

- $1/2$ CUP PLAIN YOGURT (NOT LOW-FAT)
- $1/2$ CUP SWEETENED SHREDDED COCONUT
- $1/4$ CUP MINCED FRESH CILANTRO
- 2 TABLESPOONS MINCED FRESH MINT
  SEA SALT AND FRESHLY GROUND PEPPER TO TASTE

Burgers

- $1^1/_2$ POUNDS GROUND CHUCK (ABOUT 20 PERCENT FAT)
- $3/4$ CUP CHOPPED SWEET ONION OR RED ONION

- $1^1/_2$ TEASPOONS GARAM MASALA
- $1^1/_2$ TEASPOONS SWEET CURRY POWDER
- $1^1/_2$ TEASPOONS COARSE SALT
- $1/2$ TEASPOON FRESHLY GROUND PEPPER
- $1/4$ TEASPOON CAYENNE PEPPER

- 4 CANNED OR FRESH PINEAPPLE RINGS
- 4 ONION BUNS
- 4 LETTUCE LEAVES (ROMAINE, BIBB, GREEN LEAF)
  CILANTRO AND MINT SPRIGS FOR GARNISH

In a medium bowl mix together the yogurt, coconut, cilantro, and mint. Season to taste with salt and pepper. Refrigerate chutney until needed.

Preheat the grill to medium-high heat. In a large bowl gently mix beef with onion, garam masala, curry powder, salt, pepper, and cayenne. Form into 4 1-inch-thick patties.

Oil grill grate. Grill burgers over direct heat until cooked through, 4–5 minutes per side. Grill pineapple slices alongside burgers for 3–4 minutes per side or until lightly charred. Remove burgers and pineapple slices from grill and toast buns, cut side down, along the outer edges of the grill for 2 minutes or until lightly toasted.

Spread a little of the chutney on the bottom half of each bun; top with a lettuce leaf, a burger, a pineapple slice, the rest of the chutney, and the top of the bun. Place burgers on plates or platter and garnish with mint and cilantro sprigs if desired. Serves 4.

NOTES

Burgers can also be broiled.

CLASSIC COMBO

Beefy Blue Cheese & Bacon Burgers
- *Replace chutney with Balsamic-Gorgonzola Onions (page 78)*
- *Omit garam masala, curry powder, and cayenne.*
- *Add 1½ tablespoons Worcestershire sauce and 2 teaspoons minced fresh garlic to beef mixture.*
- *Replace pineapple with cooked, thick-cut bacon; 2 slices per burger.*
- *Garnish with rosemary and thyme sprigs.*

DARING PAIRING

Chile-Fired Burgers with Chimichurri
- *Replace chutney with Chimichurri Sauce (page 104)*
- *Omit garam masala, curry powder, salt and pepper.*
- *Add 2½ tablespoons Southwest Spice Rub (page 34), 1 teaspoon dried oregano and*
- *1 tablespoon Worcestershire sauce to beef mixture.*
- *Omit pineapple.*
- *Spread 1 tablespoon bottled chili sauce (such as Bennett's) on the bottom half of each bun.*
- *Garnish with Italian parsley sprigs.*
- *If using a purchased southwest spice mix, be sure to check the salt level and package directions, and adjust accordingly.*

Provençal Grilled Lamb Chops with Lemon-Tarragon Aioli

Look for the meatiest chops you can find and take care not to overcook. Lamb chops are at their succulent best when they are pink and juicy on the inside. If you're not a fan of lamb, bone-in rib pork chops or pork tenderloin would also work well here.

Provençal Herb Paste

2   tablespoons extra virgin olive oil

2   tablespoons minced fresh rosemary

1½ tablespoons minced fresh thyme

1   tablespoon minced fresh tarragon

1   teaspoon minced fresh garlic

½   teaspoon chopped dried lavender buds

8   large, meaty lamb chops (about 2 to 2½ pounds)

Lemon-Tarragon Aioli

½   cup mayonnaise

1   medium shallot, chopped

1½ tablespoons fresh lemon juice

1   teaspoon grated lemon zest

2   tablespoons chopped fresh tarragon

1½ teaspoons minced fresh garlic

1½ teaspoons Dijon mustard

Sea salt and freshly ground pepper

Rosemary, thyme, and tarragon sprigs for garnish

In a small bowl combine olive oil, rosemary, thyme, tarragon, garlic, and lavender. Trim fat from lamb chops, leaving a thin layer. Spread herb paste all over chops and refrigerate, covered, for 2–4 hours.

Meanwhile, make aioli. In a mini-processor or blender combine the mayonnaise, shallot, lemon juice, lemon zest, tarragon, garlic, and mustard and purée. Season to taste with salt and pepper. Refrigerate until needed.

Preheat the grill to medium-high heat. Oil grill grates. Remove lamb chops from herb paste and sprinkle with salt and pepper. Grill, over direct heat, about 4 minutes per side for medium rare, or to desired degree of doneness.

Remove chops to platter or plates and drizzle with aioli. Pass remaining aioli separately. Garnish with herb sprigs if desired. Serves 4.

Notes

Lamb chops can also be broiled.

CLASSIC COMBO

Mediterranean Lamb Chops with Cucumber-Fennel Tzatziki
- *Replace herb paste with Mediterranean Red Wine Marinade (page 26).*
- *Replace aioli with Cucumber-Fennel Tzatziki (page 76).*
- *Garnish with mint or oregano sprigs.*

DARING PAIRING

Orange Infused Lamb Chops with Cranberry-Port Sauce
- *Replace herb paste with Red Wine-Orange Marinade (page 26).*
- *Replace aioli with Cranberry-Port Sauce (page 94).*
- *You will need to make the sauce after removing the chops from the marinade. Keep chops refrigerated until ready to grill.*
- *Garnish with thyme sprigs.*

Lamb Tikka with Pineapple-Coconut Raita

As you'll see here, lamb is delicious with a wide variety of ethnic seasonings and sauces. Shake things up and try all three variations with pork or beef also!

Pineapple-Coconut Raita

1/2 CUP PLAIN YOGURT (NOT FAT FREE)

1/2 CUP CHOPPED PINEAPPLE

1/2 CUP SHREDDED SWEETENED COCONUT

1/4 CUP CHOPPED FRESH CILANTRO

2 TABLESPOONS CHOPPED FRESH MINT
SEA SALT AND FRESHLY GROUND PEPPER

Spice Mix

1 1/2 TEASPOONS GARAM MASALA

1 TEASPOON CURRY POWDER

1 1/2 TEASPOONS COARSE SEA SALT OR KOSHER SALT

1/2 TEASPOON FRESHLY GROUND PEPPER

1 1/2 POUNDS BONELESS LEG OF LAMB, CUT INTO 1-INCH CHUNKS

2 TABLESPOONS CHOPPED FRESH CILANTRO
CILANTRO AND MINT SPRIGS FOR GARNISH

In a small bowl combine yogurt, pineapple, coconut, cilantro, and mint. Mix well and season to taste with salt and pepper. Set aside to allow flavors to blend.

Preheat the grill to medium-high heat.

Combine garam masala, curry powder, coarse salt, and pepper in a large ziplock bag. Add lamb and toss to coat evenly. Thread lamb onto eight long metal skewers.

Grill lamb, over direct heat, to medium rare, about 8 minutes, turning frequently.

Remove skewers to plates or platter. Sprinkle with remaining cilantro and serve with Pineapple-Coconut Raita. Garnish with cilantro and mint sprigs if desired. Serves 4.

Notes

Skewers can also be broiled.

Classic Combo

Lamb Souvlaki with Fennel & Sun-Dried Tomato Tzatziki
- *Replace raita with Fennel & Sun-Dried Tomato Tzatziki (page 77).*
- *Replace spice mix with Peppered Greek Marinade (page 22); marinate lamb for 2–4 hours prior to grilling.*

- *Pat lamb dry after removing from marinade and sprinkle lightly with salt and pepper.*
- *Replace chopped cilantro with Italian parsley.*
- *Garnish with Italian parsley sprigs.*

DARING PAIRING

Moroccan-Spiced Lamb Kabobs with Curried Orange-Apricot Sauce
- *Replace raita with Curried Orange-Apricot Sauce (page 102), spooned over kabobs.*
- *Replace spices with 1 teaspoon ground coriander, 1 teaspoon ground cumin, $\frac{1}{2}$ teaspoon ground ginger, $\frac{1}{2}$ teaspoon dried mint, plus coarse salt and pepper as above.*
- *Garnish with cilantro sprigs.*

ROASTED LEG OF LAMB WITH RED WINE-PORT SAUCE

This luscious roast lamb would be an impressive centerpiece for a dinner party. You'll want to uncork your best California Cabernet or Bordeaux to serve your guests.

SCARBOROUGH FAIR MARINADE

$1^1/_2$ CUPS DRY RED WINE

$^1/_2$ CUP MINCED SHALLOTS

$^1/_4$ CUP EXTRA VIRGIN OLIVE OIL

1 TABLESPOON MINCED FRESH GARLIC

$1^1/_2$ TABLESPOONS EACH, MINCED FRESH ITALIAN PARSLEY, SAGE, ROSEMARY AND THYME

1 TEASPOON MUSTARD SEED

1 TEASPOON COARSE SEA SALT OR KOSHER SALT

1 TEASPOON FRESHLY GROUND PEPPER

1 BUTTERFLIED, BONELESS LEG OF LAMB, ABOUT 4–$4^1/_2$ POUNDS

2 TABLESPOONS OLIVE OIL

COARSE SALT AND FRESHLY GROUND PEPPER

RED WINE-PORT SAUCE

1 CUP RUBY PORT

1 CUP LOW-SODIUM BEEF BROTH OR HOMEMADE STOCK

1 CUP LOW-SODIUM CHICKEN BROTH OR HOMEMADE STOCK

2 TABLESPOONS UNSALTED BUTTER, SOFTENED

$1^1/_2$ TABLESPOONS FLOUR

1 TABLESPOON CURRANT JELLY

PARSLEY, SAGE, ROSEMARY AND THYME SPRIGS FOR GARNISH

In a medium bowl combine all marinade ingredients. Whisk. Open up leg of lamb and place in a large, heavy-duty ziplock bag. Add marinade and place in the refrigerator for 4–12 hours, turning occasionally.

Preheat oven to 450°. Remove lamb from the bag, reserving marinade, and pat dry with paper towels. Sprinkle inside of lamb leg generously with salt and pepper. Re-roll leg and tie in 5 or 6 spots with kitchen string. Rub outside of lamb with olive oil and sprinkle generously with salt and pepper.

Place lamb on a rack in a roasting pan and roast in the middle of the oven for 1 hour, or until internal temperature reaches 125° for medium rare. Remove lamb to cutting board, tent loosely with foil, and allow to rest for 10 minutes.

While lamb roasts, make the sauce. Strain the marinade into a medium saucepan and discard the solids. Add port, bring to a boil, and boil over medium-high heat until reduced to 1 cup, about 13–15 minutes, skimming any foam. Add beef broth and chicken broth. Return to a boil and boil over medium-high heat until reduced to $1^1/_2$ cups, about 17–20 minutes. Mash together butter and flour and whisk into sauce; reduce heat to medium and cook for 2 minutes. Reduce heat to low and whisk in currant jelly. Keep warm over low heat.

Remove strings from lamb; slice into $1/2$-inch slices; fan out on platter or plates and top with sauce. Garnish with herb sprigs if desired. Serves 6.

CLASSIC COMBOS

Tuscan Herb Roasted Leg of Lamb
- *Omit marinade and sauce.*
- *Rub inside of lamb with Tuscan Herb Paste (page 30).*
- *Re-roll leg, tie and continue as directed.*

Mediterranean Lamb Roast with Greek Salsa
- *Replace marinade with Mediterranean Red Wine Marinade (page 26).*
- *Replace sauce with Greek Salsa (page 72) spooned atop sliced lamb.*

DARING PAIRING

Sweet & Savory Stuffed Lamb Roast
- *Omit marinade and sauce.*
- *Heat 2 tablespoons olive oil in a medium skillet, over medium high heat and add $1/2$ cup each: chopped pancetta, shallots, dried apricots and dried figs, plus 1 tablespoon chopped garlic. Saute for 5 minutes. Add $1/2$ cup medium dry sherry or Madeira and cook until liquid is absorbed. Stir in $1/4$ cup pine nuts. Cool slightly.*
- *After sprinkling inside of leg with salt and pepper, scatter fruit mixture plus 1 tablespoon each: chopped fresh rosemary, thyme and Italian parsley evenly over meat.*
- *Re-roll leg, tie and continue as directed.*

Greek-Style Braised Lamb Shanks

Lamb shanks are delicious and inexpensive. You may need to purchase them frozen, so be sure to plan ahead. As with the other braised recipes, the lamb shanks will be even more flavorful if braised one day in advance. Add the final toppings after reheating.

HERB/SPICE MIX

3 TEASPOONS DRIED OREGANO (GREEK OR TURKISH)

2 TEASPOONS DRIED MINT

2 TEASPOONS GROUND CORIANDER

1 TABLESPOON MINCED FRESH ROSEMARY

4 LAMB SHANKS, TRIMMED OF EXCESS FAT AS DESIRED

  COARSE SALT AND FRESHLY GROUND PEPPER

2 TABLESPOONS OLIVE OIL, MORE AS NEEDED

1 LARGE ONION, CHOPPED

2 CARROTS, PEELED AND CHOPPED

1 CELERY RIB, CHOPPED

2 TABLESPOONS CHOPPED FRESH GARLIC

1 TABLESPOON DOUBLE CONCENTRATED TOMATO PASTE (OR 2 TABLESPOONS REGULAR)

1 CUP DRY WHITE WINE, DIVIDED

2 TABLESPOONS FLOUR

1 CAN PETITE DICED TOMATOES, UNDRAINED

11 CUPS CHICKEN BROTH OR HOMEMADE STOCK

1/4 CUP PLUS 2 TABLESPOONS CHOPPED ITALIAN PARSLEY, DIVIDED

2 BAY LEAVES (MEDITERRANEAN)

OPTIONAL TOPPINGS: FETA CHEESE, KALAMATA OLIVES, LEMON ZEST, TOASTED PINE NUTS

Preheat oven to 375°. In a ramekin combine the herb/spice mix ingredients and set aside. Sprinkle lamb shanks generously with salt and pepper. Rub about 1 tablespoon of the herb/spice mix over the shanks.

In a large, heavy Dutch oven heat 2 tablespoons olive oil over medium-high heat. Add 2 of the lamb shanks and cook until nicely browned all over, about 12 minutes. Remove and repeat with remaining 2 shanks. Remove from pan and set aside.

Reduce heat to medium. Add additional olive oil if the pan seems dry, then add onion, carrots, celery, and garlic and sauté until the vegetables are soft, about 10 minutes, scraping up the browned bits from the bottom of the pan as the vegetables release their liquid. Stir in the remaining herb/spice mix and cook for 1 minute. Stir in the tomato paste and about 1/2 cup of the wine and cook until the liquid has evaporated, about 2 minutes. Sprinkle the flour over the vegetables and cook, stirring, for 30 seconds. Stir in the remaining wine, tomatoes, broth, 1/4 cup parsley and bay leaves, along with the lamb shanks and any accumulated juices. Bring to a boil. Cover the pan with a tight fitting lid and place in the oven to braise for 2 hours. Check after 10 minutes to make sure the liquid is at a steady simmer. Check once or twice during the last hour to make sure the sauce isn't sticking to the bottom of the pan, adding more chicken broth if necessary.

Remove pan from oven; remove shanks to large shallow bowls and spoon sauce over. Sprinkle with remaining 2 tablespoons parsley and optional toppings as desired. Serves 4.

CLASSIC COMBO

Moroccan Braised Lamb Shanks

- *Replace herb/spice mix with 2 teaspoons ground ginger, 1½ teaspoons cinnamon, 1½ teaspoons ground coriander and 1½ teaspoons ground cumin.*
- *Replace wine with dry (Fino or Manzanilla) sherry.*
- *Add 1 cup chopped dried apricots, along with the tomatoes and other liquids.*
- *Replace Optional Toppings with toasted sliced almonds and/or chopped, preserved lemon if desired.*

DARING PAIRING

Ancho-Cherry Braised Lamb Shanks

- *Replace herb/spice mix with 2 tablespoons Ancho chile powder, 1 teaspoon ground cinnamon, 2 teaspoons ground cumin and 1 tablespoon minced fresh thyme leaves.*
- *Replace tomato paste with 2 tablespoons balsamic vinegar.*
- *Replace wine with 1½ cups Ruby Port.*
- *Omit canned tomatoes.*
- *Reduce chicken broth to 1 cup and add 1½ cups beef broth.*
- *Add 1 cup dried, tart cherries along with the broth.*
- *Replace Optional Toppings with minced scallions or chives, toasted pumpkin seeds and/or toasted pine nuts if desired.*

SIDE DISHES

All of the recipes in this section can be partially prepared in advance, making them perfect for entertaining. With the wide variety of flavors represented in these recipes, you will easily find some that complement your entrée to a tee!

These side dishes will also add life to a simple weeknight meal of pork chops or meat loaf. Try one of the many carrot variations for an easy, colorful and delicious addition to almost any entrée.

As with all the recipes in the book, feel free to experiment. If you like the Greek-Style Green Beans, why not substitute broccoli or asparagus? Or how about replacing half of the carrots in any of the glazed carrot recipes with parsnips or sugar snap peas? The possibilities are endless!

MIXED GREEN SALADS

Any of the salads below would make a tasty first course for your next dinner party, but are simple enough to accompany any weeknight meal. For the most flavorful salad, choose a recipe based on which fruits are in season and remember to use only the best quality oils, vinegars, nuts and cheeses. Mix and match ingredients and vinaigrettes for your own signature salad!

For all of the salad combinations below, follow these simple directions:

Place all vinaigrette ingredients, except oil, in a clean glass jar; cover tightly and shake vigorously to combine. Add oil and shake until emulsified. Season vinaigrette to taste with sea salt and freshly ground pepper. Refrigerate until needed, up to 2 days.

Divide about 8 cups of your favorite mixed greens between 4 salad plates. Top greens with fruit, drizzle with vinaigrette, sprinkle with remaining ingredients, and top with a few grindings of pepper. Serve with a warm, crusty baguette accompanied by Shallot-Herb Butter (page 56) if desired. Serves 4.

CLASSIC COMBOS

Apple-Walnut Salad with Cider Vinaigrette

VINAIGRETTE INGREDIENTS:

- 3/4 CUP APPLE CIDER BOILED DOWN TO 3 TABLESPOONS AND COOLED
- 1 MINCED SHALLOT
- 1 TABLESPOON WHITE WINE VINEGAR
- 1 TABLESPOON GRAINY DIJON MUSTARD
- 3 TABLESPOONS EXTRA VIRGIN OLIVE OIL
- 3 TABLESPOONS WALNUT OIL

SALAD INGREDIENTS:

- 1 LARGE SWEET-TART APPLE, CORED AND CUT INTO 16 SLICES
- 1/2 CUP TOASTED WALNUTS
- 3 OUNCES AGED GRUYÈRE CHEESE, CUT INTO SMALL CUBES
- 2 SLICES COOKED, CRUMBLED BACON

Pear-Pecan Salad with Cider Vinaigrette

VINAIGRETTE INGREDIENTS:

3/4 CUP PEAR CIDER OR APPLE CIDER BOILED DOWN TO 3 TABLESPOONS AND COOLED

1 MINCED SHALLOT

1 TABLESPOON WHITE WINE VINEGAR

1 TABLESPOON GRAINY DIJON MUSTARD
   PINCH GROUND GINGER

3 TABLESPOONS EXTRA VIRGIN OLIVE OIL

3 TABLESPOONS HAZELNUT OIL OR WALNUT OIL

SALAD INGREDIENTS:

2 RIPE PEARS, CORED, EACH CUT INTO 8 SLICES

1/2 CUP TOASTED PECANS

2 OUNCES GORGONZOLA OR OTHER BLUE CHEESE, CRUMBLED

2 SLICES COOKED, CRUMBLED BACON

DARING PAIRINGS

Orange & Fig Salad with Sherry-Walnut Vinaigrette

VINAIGRETTE INGREDIENTS:

2 TABLESPOONS SHERRY VINEGAR

1 MINCED SHALLOT

2 TEASPOONS GRAINY DIJON MUSTARD

1/2 TABLESPOON HONEY

1/4 CUP EXTRA VIRGIN OLIVE OIL

2 TABLESPOONS WALNUT OIL

SALAD INGREDIENTS:

1 TO 2 ORANGES, PEELED AND SLICED INTO ROUNDS

8 DRIED FIGS, QUARTERED*

1/2 CUP TOASTED WALNUTS

2 OUNCES FRESH GOAT CHEESE, CRUMBLED

1/2 CUP POMEGRANATE SEEDS (OPTIONAL)

*IF FRESH FIGS ARE IN SEASON, GIVE THEM A TRY HERE.

Summer Strawberry Salad

VINAIGRETTE INGREDIENTS:

2 TABLESPOONS BALSAMIC VINEGAR

1/2 TABLESPOON FRESH LEMON JUICE

1 MINCED SHALLOT

1/2 TABLESPOON GRAINY DIJON MUSTARD

1/2 TABLESPOON DIJON MUSTARD

1/2 TABLESPOON HONEY

6 TABLESPOONS EXTRA VIRGIN OLIVE OIL

SALAD INGREDIENTS:

1 CUP SLICED STRAWBERRIES

1/4 CUP TOASTED PINE NUTS

2 TO 3 OUNCES FETA CHEESE, CRUMBLED

2 OUNCES PROSCIUTTO, CUT INTO THIN STRIPS AND SAUTÉED IN A LITTLE OLIVE OIL UNTIL CRISP

Pac-Rim Mango Salad

1/2 CUP GINGER-LIME VINAIGRETTE (PAGE 116)

SALAD INGREDIENTS:

1 MANGO, CUBED

1 THINLY SLICED ASIAN PEAR OR 1 CUP THINLY SLICED SEEDLESS CUCUMBER

1/2 CUP ROASTED, SALTED CASHEWS

ROASTED VEGETABLE PANZANELLA

Panzanella is a classic Italian grilled bread salad. Here I've added lots of tasty roasted vegetables and toasted the bread in the oven for convenience. Rather than giving Classic Combos and Daring Pairings, I'm giving you a variety of possible ingredient substitutions to take this salad and Make It Your Own!

SALAD

1   LARGE RED BELL PEPPER, QUARTERED, RIBS AND SEEDS REMOVED

1   MEDIUM RED ONION, PEELED AND CUT INTO 8 WEDGES

1   LARGE FENNEL BULB, TRIMMED AND CUT INTO 8 WEDGES

4   TABLESPOONS OLIVE OIL, DIVIDED
SEA SALT AND FRESHLY GROUND PEPPER TO TASTE

4   1-INCH THICK SLICES ITALIAN COUNTRY-STYLE BREAD

1   GARLIC CLOVE, PEELED AND HALVED LENGTHWISE

1   MEDIUM CUCUMBER, QUARTERED LENGTHWISE, SEEDED AND SLICED $1/2$ INCH THICK

2   MEDIUM RIPE RED TOMATOES, SEEDED AND CUT INTO BITE-SIZED PIECES

$1/4$ CUP TORN FRESH BASIL LEAVES

$1/4$ CUP ITALIAN PARSLEY LEAVES

$1/4$ CUP MEDITERRANEAN-STYLE BLACK OLIVES, PITTED AND HALVED

$1/2$ CUP CRUMBLED RICOTTA SALATA OR FETA CHEESE

VINAIGRETTE

2   TEASPOONS RED WINE VINEGAR

2   TEASPOONS FRESH LEMON JUICE

$1/2$ TEASPOON SUGAR

1   TEASPOON DIJON MUSTARD

4   TABLESPOONS EXTRA VIRGIN OLIVE OIL
SEA SALT AND FRESHLY GROUND PEPPER TO TASTE

Preheat oven to 400°. On a large heavy baking sheet brush red pepper, onion, and fennel with 2 tablespoons olive oil and season with salt and pepper. Roast in oven for 20 minutes. Turn vegetables over and roast for an additional 20 minutes or until lightly browned and softened. Remove from oven and cut into bite-sized pieces.

During last 10 minutes of roasting, brush bread slices with remaining 2 tablespoons olive oil and bake, directly on oven rack, for 5 minutes per side or until nicely toasted. Remove bread from oven and rub one side of slices with cut sides of garlic clove. Cut bread into bite-sized chunks.

In a small bowl whisk together red wine vinegar, lemon juice, sugar, and mustard. Whisk in olive oil. Season vinaigrette to taste with salt and pepper.

Place roasted vegetables, cucumber, tomato, basil, and parsley in a large bowl. Add half of the vinaigrette and toss to coat. Add the bread chunks, olives, cheese, and remaining vinaigrette and toss again. Serve immediately. Serves 4.

MAKE IT YOUR OWN

- For the vegetables to be roasted, substitute: portabella or cremini mushrooms; green, yellow or orange peppers; zucchini or summer squash; eggplant.
- For the Italian bread, substitute: onion-dill bread, rosemary-olive oil bread, roasted garlic bread, foccacia, or sourdough.
- For the cucumbers, substitute: diced jicama; blanched, shelled edamame; water chestnuts; thinly sliced carrot.
- For the herbs, substitute: chives; arugula; watercress; dill.
- For the olives, substitute: capers; pepperoncini; artichoke hearts; pickled garlic; other olives such as Niçoise, Luques or your favorite.
- For the cheese, substitute: goat cheese or herbed goat cheese; queso fresco; cubes of fresh mozzarella, Gruyère, Fontina, or Provolone; fresh Parmesan shavings.
- Other possible additions: toasted pine nuts; pistachios; chopped and sautéed prosciutto, pancetta or bacon; chopped hard-boiled egg.

Pesto Stuffed Baked Potatoes

These stuffed potatoes are delicious and look great on the plate beside your entrée. Since the fillings are so rich and flavorful, one-half potato is the perfect serving size; but go ahead and make extras if you're feeding big eaters!

4 LARGE BAKING POTATOES (RUSSET, IDAHO)
1/4 CUP EXTRA VIRGIN OLIVE OIL
1 TO 2 TABLESPOONS COARSE SALT
2 TABLESPOONS UNSALTED BUTTER
1/2 CUP WHOLE MILK OR HALF & HALF, MORE AS NEEDED

1/4 CUP BASIL-MINT PESTO (PAGE 104 OR STORE-BOUGHT BASIL PESTO)
1 TABLESPOON ROASTED GARLIC (PAGE 8 OR STORE-BOUGHT)
1/2 CUP CRUMBLED GOAT CHEESE
SEA SALT AND FRESHLY GROUND PEPPER TO TASTE

Preheat oven to 450°. Scrub potatoes. Rub with oil and coarse salt. Bake directly on oven rack for 1 hour. Remove and reduce oven temperature to 400°.

When potatoes are cool enough to handle, cut in half crosswise. Scoop out halves, leaving a 1/4-inch shell, and cut a little slice off of the ends so that potatoes will stand upright.

Put potato flesh through a ricer or mash by hand. Mix in the butter, milk, pesto, garlic, and goat cheese, adding more milk as needed to achieve desired consistency. Season to taste with salt and pepper. Stuff potato mixture back into shells; place on a baking sheet and return to the oven for 20–25 minutes. Serves 8.

Notes

For each of the following options, replace the pesto, garlic, and goat cheese with the ingredients listed.

Classic Combo

Bacon & Cheddar Stuffed Potatoes
4 slices cooked and crumbled bacon, 1 cup shredded Cheddar cheese, 1/4 cup minced fresh chives

DARING PAIRINGS

Blue Cheese, Pancetta & Mushroom Stuffed Potatoes
½ cup blue cheese, ½ cup chopped and sautéed mushrooms, 3 ounces chopped and sautéed pancetta

Southwestern Stuffed Potatoes
1 cup shredded pepper-jack cheese, 1 teaspoon ground cumin, ¼ cup chopped roasted red peppers (page 9 or store-bought)

Rosemary & Gruyère Stuffed Potatoes
2 tablespoons minced fresh rosemary, 1 cup shredded Gruyère cheese, ½ teaspoon ground nutmeg

Roasted Garlic Smashed Potatoes

Who doesn't love mashed potatoes? This savory version is particularly delicious and, if you keep some roasted garlic on hand, a snap to prepare as well! All of the variations here can be made an hour or two in advance and left in the pot, covered, at room temperature. Reheat gently and add a little extra milk, if needed, to achieve desired consistency.

2½ POUNDS RED SKINNED POTATOES OR YUKON
    GOLD POTATOES, SCRUBBED AND CUT INTO
    2-INCH PIECES
    COARSE SEA SALT OR KOSHER SALT
½ CUP HALF AND HALF OR WHOLE MILK
¼ CUP MINCED SCALLIONS

¼ CUP UNSALTED BUTTER, SOFTENED
2 TABLESPOONS SOUR CREAM
2 TABLESPOONS ROASTED GARLIC (PAGE 8 OR
    STORE-BOUGHT)
    SEA SALT AND FRESHLY GROUND PEPPER TO
    TASTE

Place potatoes in a large, heavy pot. Cover with cold water and season with coarse salt. Bring to a boil over medium-high heat and boil until very tender, about 20 minutes.

Drain potatoes. Return to pot and cook over medium-low heat for 1–2 minutes to evaporate excess moisture. Reduce heat to low, add remaining ingredients to pot, and mash with a hand held potato masher. Season to taste with salt and pepper. Serves 6.

Classic Combo

Pancetta & Leek Smashed Potatoes
    Sauté 2 ounces chopped pancetta and 1½ cups halved and thinly sliced leek in 1 table-
    spoon butter, over medium heat, until lightly browned. Stir into Roasted Garlic
    Smashed Potatoes.

Daring Pairings

Wild Mushroom Smashed Potatoes

Stir ½ to 1 recipe Wild Mushroom Saute (page 86) into Roasted Garlic Smashed Potatoes.

Southwest Corn Smashed Potatoes

Stir ½ to 1 recipe Smoky Southwestern Corn Salsa (page 60) into Roasted Garlic Smashed Potatoes.

Twice-Baked Sweet Potatoes with Maple-Bourbon Butter

Not just for holidays, sweet potatoes are a delicious accompaniment to all types of entrées. The variations here should give you some idea as to their versatility! Potatoes can be baked and stuffed up to 2 hours in advance and left at room temperature. Increase the twice-baking time by about 10 minutes.

6   ORANGE-FLESHED SWEET POTATOES (YAMS)
1   TABLESPOON OLIVE OIL OR VEGETABLE OIL
1   STICK UNSALTED BUTTER, SOFTENED, DIVIDED
1   BUNCH SCALLIONS, MINCED
1   TEASPOON GRATED FRESH ORANGE ZEST, OR $1/2$ TEASPOON DRIED

$1/2$ TEASPOON GROUND CINNAMON
$1/4$ TEASPOON GROUND ALLSPICE
$1/4$ TEASPOON GROUND NUTMEG
$1/8$ TEASPOON CAYENNE PEPPER
$1/4$ CUP KENTUCKY BOURBON
$1^1/2$ TABLESPOONS PURE MAPLE SYRUP
  SEA SALT AND FRESHLY GROUND PEPPER

Preheat oven to 425°. Scrub the potatoes and rub with the oil. Place on a foil-lined baking sheet. Poke a few holes in the potatoes to vent. Bake until a knife slips easily into the center of the potatoes, about 50–60 minutes. Remove to a rack to cool slightly. Maintain oven temperature.

Meanwhile make butter. In a small saucepan heat 1 tablespoon butter over medium heat. Add half of the scallions and sauté for 2 minutes. Add orange zest, cinnamon, allspice, nutmeg, and cayenne and sauté for 1 minute. Add bourbon and cook for 2 minutes or until evaporated. Add maple syrup and cook for 2 minutes. Remove from heat. Cool slightly, then mix with remaining butter.

When the potatoes are cool enough to handle, slice off the top third of the potatoes (horizontally.) Scoop the potato flesh into a large bowl. Leave about a $1/4$-inch border of potato in the bottom shell, to retain its shape. Discard the skin from the tops of potatoes.

Mix Maple-Bourbon Butter into potato flesh and season to taste with salt and pepper. Spoon potato flesh back into shells, return to baking sheet and bake for an additional 20 minutes.

Remove to dinner plates or platter; sprinkle with remaining scallions and serve. Serves 6.

Classic Combos

Twice-Baked Sweet Potatoes with Orange-Honey Butter
- *Sauté 1 tablespoon minced fresh ginger along with scallions.*
- *Omit cinnamon and nutmeg.*
- *Add ¼ teaspoon ground cloves with allspice and cayenne.*
- *Replace bourbon with fresh orange juice.*
- *Replace maple syrup with honey.*

Twice-Baked Sweet Potatoes with Smoky Chipotle Butter
- *Bake potatoes according to directions above.*
- *Mix potato flesh with Smoky Chipotle Butter (page 52), softened.*
- *Season to taste with salt and pepper.*
- *Sprinkle finished potatoes with 2 tablespoons minced scallions.*

Daring Pairings

Ginger & Sesame Twice-Baked Sweet Potatoes
- *Sauté 1½ tablespoons minced fresh ginger and 1 tablespoon minced fresh garlic along with scallions.*
- *Omit cinnamon, allspice and nutmeg.*
- *Replace bourbon with medium dry sherry.*
- *Replace maple syrup with 1 tablespoon Asian sesame oil and 2 teaspoons toasted sesame seeds.*

Moroccan Spiced Sweet Potatoes with Lemon-Honey Butter
- *Sauté 1 tablespoon minced fresh ginger and 2 teaspoons minced fresh garlic along with scallions.*
- *Replace orange zest with lemon zest.*
- *Omit allspice and nutmeg.*
- *Add ½ teaspoon ground cumin and ½ teaspoon ground coriander with cinnamon and cayenne.*
- *Replace bourbon with 3 tablespoons lemon juice.*
- *Replace maple syrup with honey.*

Twice-Baked Sweet Potatoes with Cilantro-Lime Butter
- *Bake potatoes according to directions above.*
- *Mix potato flesh with Cilantro-Lime Butter (page 56), softened.*
- *Season to taste with salt and pepper.*
- *Fill and twice bake potatoes according to directions above.*
- *Sprinkle finished potatoes with 2 tablespoons minced scallions.*

CRUNCHY SPICED OVEN-ROASTED CORN

You won't believe how delicious corn on the cob is when prepared this way; tender and crisp all in one bite! It's the perfect side dish for a backyard barbecue, when your grill is being used for other things. Coat and bread the corn early in the day, then place on a baking sheet, cover loosely with plastic wrap, and refrigerate until 30 minutes before you're ready to roast.

$1/2$ CUP MAYONNAISE

$1/4$ CUP MINCED SCALLIONS, WHITE AND GREEN PARTS

2 TABLESPOONS ALEPPO PEPPER

$1^1/2$ TABLESPOONS ROASTED GARLIC (PAGE 8 OR STORE BOUGHT)

1 TABLESPOON FRESH LEMON JUICE

1 TEASPOON SEA SALT

6 EARS CORN, SHUCKED

4 CUPS FRESH BREADCRUMBS

Preheat oven to 400°. In a medium bowl whisk together the mayonnaise, scallions, Aleppo pepper, roasted garlic, lemon juice, and salt. Brush mayonnaise mixture evenly over corn, then coat corn thoroughly with breadcrumbs. Place on a baking sheet and bake for 30 minutes or until golden brown and crisp. Serves 6.

CLASSIC COMBO

Southwest-Spiced Oven-Roasted Corn

Whisk ½ cup mayonnaise with ¼ cup minced scallions, ¼ cup minced cilantro, grated zest and 2 tablespoons juice from 1 lime, 1 tablespoon minced fresh garlic, 2 teaspoons Southwest Spice Rub (page 34), ½ teaspoon sea salt and ¼ teaspoon pepper. Proceed with coating and baking corn as above.

DARING PAIRINGS

Asian Oven-Roasted Corn

Whisk ½ cup mayonnaise with ¼ cup minced scallions, 2 tablespoons minced cilantro, 2 tablespoons minced fresh basil, 1 tablespoon fresh lime juice, 1 tablespoon toasted sesame oil, 1 tablespoon minced fresh garlic, 1 teaspoon grated fresh ginger, 1 teaspoon sea salt and ½ teaspoon pepper. Proceed with coating and baking corn as above.

Oven-Roasted Corn Italiano

Whisk ½ cup mayonnaise with ¼ cup freshly grated Parmesan cheese, 2 tablespoons minced shallots, 2 tablespoons minced Italian parsley, 2 tablespoons minced fresh basil, 1 tablespoon minced fresh garlic, 1 tablespoon fresh lemon juice, 1 teaspoon sea salt, ¼ teaspoon pepper and ¼ teaspoon red pepper flakes. Proceed with coating and baking corn as above.

Orange-Spice Glazed Carrots & Shallots

Glazed carrots are a colorful addition to most any dinner plate. I went a little crazy with variations here; but I'm confident that you can still come up with a few more of your own!

2   TABLESPOONS UNSALTED BUTTER

1/2 POUND SHALLOTS, PEELED, HALVED IF SMALL OR QUARTERED IF LARGE

1/4 TEASPOON EACH GROUND CUMIN, CORIANDER AND ALLSPICE

1/2 CUP FRESH ORANGE JUICE

1/2 CUP CHICKEN OR VEGETABLE BROTH

1   TABLESPOON LIGHT BROWN SUGAR

1   TEASPOON KOSHER SALT

1 1/2 POUNDS CARROTS, PEELED AND CUT INTO 1/2-INCH THICK DIAGONAL SLICES

SEA SALT AND FRESHLY GROUND PEPPER (OPTIONAL)

2   TABLESPOONS MINCED FRESH CILANTRO

In a 10- or 12-inch sauté pan melt butter over medium-high heat. Add shallots and sauté for 3 minutes or until golden brown. Add spices and cook, stirring, for 1 minute. Stir in orange juice, broth, brown sugar, salt, and carrots. Bring to a boil, partially cover pan, reduce heat, and simmer for 10 minutes. Uncover pan. Increase heat slightly and continue to simmer, stirring occasionally, until carrots are tender and liquid has reduced to a glaze, about 8 more minutes. Season to taste with additional salt and pepper if desired. Sprinkle with cilantro. Serves 4.

Classic Combos

Orange-Fennel Glazed Carrots & Shallots
- *Replace spices with 2 teaspoons crushed fennel seeds.*
- *Replace brown sugar with sugar.*
- *Replace cilantro with fresh tarragon or Italian parsley.*

Marsala Glazed Carrots & Shallots
- *Omit spices.*
- *Replace orange juice with sweet Marsala.*
- *Omit brown sugar.*
- *Replace cilantro with 1/4 cup chopped Italian parsley.*

Maple-Mustard Glazed Carrots & Shallots
- *Replace spices with 2 teaspoons mustard seeds.*
- *Replace orange juice with 1/4 cup Bourbon.*
- *Increase broth to 3/4 cup.*
- *Replace brown sugar with 1 1/2 tablespoons pure maple syrup.*
- *Omit cilantro.*

Apple Cider Glazed Carrots & Shallots
- *Replace spices with $1/2$ teaspoon ground cinnamon.*
- *Replace orange juice with apple cider.*
- *Replace cilantro with Italian parsley or omit.*

Daring Pairings

Honey-Lime Glazed Carrots & Shallots
- *Replace spices with 1 teaspoon ground ginger or 2 teaspoons minced fresh ginger.*
- *Replace orange juice with 3 tablespoons fresh lime juice plus $1/2$ teaspoon grated lime zest.*
- *Increase broth to $3/4$ cup.*
- *Replace brown sugar with $1 1/2$ tablespoons honey.*

Lemon-Clove Glazed Carrots & Shallots
- *Replace spices with $1/2$ teaspoon ground cloves.*
- *Replace orange juice with 3 tablespoons fresh lemon juice plus 1 teaspoon grated lemon zest.*
- *Increase broth to $3/4$ cup.*
- *Replace brown sugar with $1 1/2$ tablespoons honey.*
- *Replace cilantro with Italian parsley.*

Tangerine-Maple Glazed Carrots & Shallots
- *Omit spices.*
- *Replace orange juice with tangerine juice.*
- *Replace brown sugar with pure maple syrup.*
- *Replace cilantro with Italian parsley.*

Maple-Rum Glazed Carrots & Shallots
- *Omit spices.*
- *Replace orange juice with $1/4$ cup spiced rum or dark rum.*
- *Increase broth to $3/4$ cup.*
- *Replace brown sugar with $1 1/2$ tablespoons pure maple syrup.*
- *Replace cilantro with $1/4$ cup chopped, toasted pecans.*

Pineapple-Rum Glazed Carrots & Shallots
- *Replace spices with 2 teaspoons minced fresh ginger.*
- *Replace orange juice with $1/4$ cup spiced rum or dark rum.*
- *Increase broth to $3/4$ cup.*
- *Replace brown sugar with 2 tablespoons pineapple preserves.*
- *Omit cilantro.*

Fancy-Schmancy Green Beans

This recipe earned me a finalist spot on Live with Regis & Kelly's *Thanksgiving Cook-Off in 2003. Regis and I prepared it for the judges, who loved it. Your friends and family will love it too!*

1 1/2 POUNDS FRESH GREEN BEANS, TRIMMED

Caramelized Onion Layer

2 TABLESPOONS UNSALTED BUTTER

2 LARGE SWEET ONIONS, HALVED VERTICALLY AND THINLY SLICED

1 TABLESPOON BALSAMIC VINEGAR

Mushroom Layer

2 OUNCES PANCETTA, CHOPPED

6 OUNCES CREMINI MUSHROOMS, SLICED

6 OUNCES SHIITAKE MUSHROOMS, STEMS REMOVED, SLICED

3/4 TEASPOON DRIED TARRAGON

1/3 CUP GOOD QUALITY DRY MARSALA

1/2 CUP WHIPPING CREAM OR HALF & HALF

SEA SALT AND FRESHLY GROUND PEPPER

2 TABLESPOONS UNSALTED BUTTER

1 TEASPOON GRATED ZEST AND 1 TABLESPOON JUICE FROM ONE LEMON

In large pot of boiling water cook beans until crisp-tender, about 5 minutes. Drain and rinse under cold water to stop the cooking. Set aside.

In a large nonstick skillet heat 2 tablespoons butter over medium heat. Add onion slices and cook, stirring frequently, until very soft and deeply caramelized, about 20 minutes. Remove from heat, stir in balsamic vinegar, and season to taste with salt and pepper. Remove onions to a small bowl. Cover to keep warm.

Wipe out skillet; add pancetta and cook over medium heat for 5 minutes or until beginning to brown. Add mushrooms and tarragon and cook until mushrooms are lightly browned and the liquid they release has evaporated, about 8–10 minutes. Add Marsala and cook until nearly evaporated, 2–3 minutes. Add cream and cook until slightly thickened, 1–2 minutes. Remove from heat and season to taste with salt and pepper.

While mushrooms are cooking, return beans to pot, along with remaining 2 tablespoons butter, and cook over medium heat until beans are warmed through and glazed with butter, 3–5 minutes.

Arrange beans on serving platter and sprinkle with salt, pepper, grated lemon zest, and lemon juice. Spoon mushroom mixture over beans, leaving about a 1/2 inch border of beans showing. Scatter onions over mushroom layer. Serves 6–8.

Notes

Mushroom mixture and caramelized onions can be made up to one day in advance. Store separately in the refrigerator. Reheat in the microwave or atop the stove. Beans can be boiled up to two days in advance, patted dry and stored in ziplock bags in the refrigerator.

Classic Combos

Green Beans with Bacon & Corn
- *Omit onion layer and mushroom layer.*
- *Top green bean layer with Pancetta-Corn Salsa (page 60).*

Green Beans with Tomatoes & Feta
- *Omit onion layer, mushroom layer, lemon zest and juice.*
- *Top green bean layer with Two-Tomato Vinaigrette (page 115).*
- *Sprinkle with crumbled Feta cheese.*

Daring Pairings

Greek-Style Green Beans
- *Omit onion layer, mushroom layer, lemon zest and juice.*
- *Top green bean layer with Greek Salsa (page 72).*

Over-the-Top Fancy-Schmancy Green Beans
- *Replace onion layer with Balsamic-Gorgonzola Onions (page 78).*

Tuscan-Inspired Green Beans
- *Omit onion layer and mushroom layer.*
- *Top green bean layer with Roasted Eggplant-Pepper Relish (page 80).*
- *Sprinkle with freshly grated Parmesan cheese.*

Citrus & Garlic Green Beans
- *Omit onion layer and mushroom layer.*
- *Sprinkle Orange-Chive Gremolata (page 88) over green bean layer.*

Sesame-Scallion Green Beans
- *Omit onion layer and mushroom layer.*
- *Sprinkle Sesame-Scallion Gremolata (page 88) over green bean layer.*

Summer Vegetable Sauté

These lively vegetable sautés will add a burst of color and flavor to any meal. Feel free to mix and match vegetables to suit your taste and the season.

3   TABLESPOONS UNSALTED BUTTER
1   MEDIUM SWEET ONION, HALVED LENGTHWISE AND THINLY SLICED
1   RED BELL PEPPER, QUARTERED, CORED AND THINLY SLICED
3   SMALL ZUCCHINI, CUT INTO $\frac{1}{3}$-INCH THICK ROUNDS
2   MEDIUM YELLOW SUMMER SQUASH, CUT INTO $\frac{1}{3}$-INCH THICK ROUNDS

2   TABLESPOONS MINCED FRESH GARLIC
2   CUPS FRESH CORN KERNELS (SUBSTITUTE FROZEN, THAWED IF DESIRED)
$\frac{1}{4}$ CUP CHOPPED ITALIAN PARSLEY
$\frac{1}{4}$ CUP DRY VERMOUTH OR WHITE WINE
    SEA SALT AND FRESHLY GROUND PEPPER
$\frac{1}{4}$ CUP JULIENNE BASIL LEAVES
1   TEASPOON GRATED LEMON ZEST (OPTIONAL)

In a large (12-inch) sauté pan heat butter over medium-high heat. Add onion and sauté for 5 minutes. Add red pepper, zucchini, yellow squash, and garlic and sauté until vegetables begin to brown, about 7 minutes. Add corn kernels and parsley and sauté for 3 minutes. Add vermouth and cook until evaporated, about 2 minutes, or until the vegetables are done to your liking.

Remove vegetables from heat and season to taste with salt and pepper. Remove to serving bowl and scatter basil and lemon zest over the top. Serves 6.

Classic Combos

Fennel-Tarragon Vegetable Sauté
- *Add 1 cored and thinly sliced fennel bulb with onion.*
- *Omit red pepper.*
- *Add 1 tablespoon fresh thyme leaves with garlic.*
- *Replace parsley with fresh tarragon.*
- *Replace basil and lemon zest with 2 tablespoons chopped fennel fronds and 1/4 cup toasted pine nuts.*

Ginger-Coconut Vegetable Sauté
- *Add 8 ounces trimmed sugar snap peas with red pepper.*
- *Add 2 tablespoons minced fresh ginger with garlic.*
- *Omit corn and parsley.*
- *Replace vermouth with $1/3$ cup coconut milk, plus 1 tablespoon lime juice.*
- *Replace basil and lemon zest with 2 tablespoons minced fresh cilantro and $1/4$ cup toasted coconut flakes.*

DARING PAIRINGS

Smoky Southwest Vegetable Sauté
- *Omit yellow squash.*
- *Add 2 roasted and chopped poblano peppers with corn.*
- *Replace parsley with fresh oregano.*
- *Replace vermouth with $1/4$ cup chicken broth, plus 1 tablespoon lime juice.*
- *Replace basil and lemon zest with $1/4$ cup chopped fresh cilantro.*

Miso-Sesame Vegetable Sauté
- *Replace 1 tablespoon butter with 1 tablespoon Asian sesame oil.*
- *Add 2 tablespoons minced fresh ginger with garlic.*
- *Replace corn with shelled edamame.*
- *Omit parsley.*
- *Replace vermouth with $1/4$ cup dry sherry whisked together with 2 tablespoons light miso.*
- *Replace basil and lemon zest with 2 tablespoons toasted sesame seeds.*

CREATIVE COUPLINGS

In this section I've provided you with a form to create your own recipes by varying the ones in this book. Mix and match the recipes to make it *your* own. You might be surprised what delicious dishes you come up with. Then visit my Website at www.jamiecooks.com and let me know what you've created!

CREATIVE COUPLINGS

BASE RECIPE: _Goat Cheese Stuffed Turkey Burgers_   PAGE 182

REPLACE _Charred pepper & onion relish_ WITH _Pancetta-Corn Salsa_   PAGE 60

REPLACE _Goat cheese filling_ WITH _Shredded smoked Cheddar_   PAGE —

NOTES: _Replace arugula with romaine or leaf lettuce_

BASE RECIPE: _____ PAGE

REPLACE _____ WITH _____ PAGE

REPLACE _____ WITH _____ PAGE

NOTES: _____

BASE RECIPE: _____ PAGE

REPLACE _____ WITH _____ PAGE

REPLACE _____ WITH _____ PAGE

NOTES: _____

BASE RECIPE: _____ PAGE

REPLACE _____ WITH _____ PAGE

REPLACE _____ WITH _____ PAGE

NOTES: _____

BASE RECIPE: _____ | PAGE |

REPLACE _____ WITH _____ | PAGE |

REPLACE _____ WITH _____ | PAGE |

NOTES: _____

_____

BASE RECIPE: _____ | PAGE |

REPLACE _____ WITH _____ | PAGE |

REPLACE _____ WITH _____ | PAGE |

NOTES: _____

_____

BASE RECIPE: _____ | PAGE |

REPLACE _____ WITH _____ | PAGE |

REPLACE _____ WITH _____ | PAGE |

NOTES: _____

_____

BASE RECIPE: _____ | PAGE |

REPLACE _____ WITH _____ | PAGE |

REPLACE _____ WITH _____ | PAGE |

NOTES: _____

_____

BASE RECIPE: _____ | PAGE

REPLACE _____ WITH _____ | PAGE

REPLACE _____ WITH _____ | PAGE

NOTES: _____

_____

BASE RECIPE: _____ | PAGE

REPLACE _____ WITH _____ | PAGE

REPLACE _____ WITH _____ | PAGE

NOTES: _____

_____

BASE RECIPE: _____ | PAGE

REPLACE _____ WITH _____ | PAGE

REPLACE _____ WITH _____ | PAGE

NOTES: _____

_____

BASE RECIPE: _____ | PAGE

REPLACE _____ WITH _____ | PAGE

REPLACE _____ WITH _____ | PAGE

NOTES: _____

_____

ACKNOWLEDGMENTS

Topping the list, I'd like to thank my best friend and husband, Greg, for his constant love and support throughout this and all my cooking endeavors.

Thank you to my parents, who've supported and encouraged me in everything I've chosen to do. Thanks to all of my friends, especially Alkis, Denise, Kim, Suzanne, Errin, and Jeff, for their fearless taste-testing, great ideas, constant encouragement, and so much more.

Thanks to everyone at Cumberland House Publishing for making this dream a reality. To Ron Pitkin for taking a chance on a first-time author. To Julie Pitkin for the beautifully designed cover. And to my editor, Mary Sanford, for somehow turning my giant three-ring binder into a real, honest-to-God cookbook!

Last but not least, I'd like to thank God for bringing me my beautiful daughter, Jade, who makes every day a great one and everything I do worthwhile.

ACKNOWLEDGMENTS

RECIPE INDEX

CATEGORY INDEX

CATEGORY INDEX

ABOUT THE AUTHOR

Jamie Miller has developed hundreds of creative recipes and has won many cooking awards, including the grand prize at the 2004 Florida Citrus Cook-Off. She has prepared her award-winning recipes on television, including *Live with Regis & Kelly* and numerous Food Network specials, where she continues to appear frequently. Many of her recipes have been published in cookbooks, newspapers, and such national magazines as *Southern Living, Cooking Pleasures,* and *Bon Appetit.* She lives in suburban Minneapolis, Minnesota.

9 781581 825930